Building a Cyber Strategy using BAP – Vol 2

Jeffrey Lush –
bapSolution.com

Second Printing: 2018

ISBN: 978-0-359-18447-7

Purchase printed book at: http://www.lulu.com Search for Jeffrey Lush

Contents

Building a Cyber Strategy using BAP – Vol 2 1

Introduction 4

Chapter 1: Achieving Cyber Accountability 5

Chapter 2: Step 1: Discover and Build Controls...................... 7

Chapter 3: Step 2: Validate Controls and Policies 10

Chapter 4: Step 3: Analyze Cyber Health 11

Chapter 5: Events and Cyber Accountability 16

Chapter 6: Cyber Health for Multiple Sites 17

Chapter 7: Remediation – POA&M 18

Chapter 8: The impact of Data Collection 20

Chapter 9: Validation and Accountability 26

Chapter 10: The "real" cost of Cyber 28

Appendix A: Firewall Breach.. 45

Appendix B: VA OIG Report 51

Appendix C: BAP Functionality 73

Glossary 95

Document ideas about your Strategy 98

Introduction

What makes **BAP** unique in an industry flooded with cybersecurity solutions? *Simple-* **BAP** is Accountable Security, developed with the end state in mind, making

Cyber and Compliance easier and accountable.

The following pages will explore cyber from the development of a strategy to validation and data collection to the cost of cyber and compliance, concluding with multiple examples and use cases within Appendix A, B, and C.

The book highlights two US Federal Organizations and practices: the US Department of Defense (DoD) and the US Department of Veteran Affairs (VA). DoD leverages a compliance regulation called the Risk Management Framework (RMF). Throughout the book, multiple references will be made to DoD, the VA, and RMF.

The US Department of Defense represents the world's largest military organization, and the US Department of Veterans Affairs is the world's largest civilian agency. Collectively they represent many, if not all the challenges of developing and implementing a successful cyber and compliance strategy.

BAP leverages existing cyber investments, augmenting the tools and information collected to bridge the gap between real-time threat detection and an organization's cyber standards, policy, and compliance. Compliance requires accountability to rules and procedures; **BAP** enables success.

It's as easy as BAP.

Chapter 1: Achieving Cyber Accountability

It is virtually impossible to declare success in the absence of defining what success is. Indeed, there is no lack of passion within cybersecurity professionals, which include professionals interested in cyber policies and controls, or cyber professionals engaged in cyber operations. Each of these groups of professionals focuses on achieving cyber strength for their environment.

The challenge in the industry: Do our efforts result in a compliant datacenter and services? Are we making it more difficult for cybercriminals?

A cyber policy is a foundational effort, the starting point for accountability within cyber operations. Without cyber controls and policy, cyber defense is less than optimal. We may be able to defend against the known or predicted cyber threat, although, without stated objectives (cyber policy), organizations limit themselves to a flat dimensional view of the cyber threat. Establishing cyber policy is a starting point and has little to do with actual cyber protection.

Cyber protection is in the execution and implementation of the cyber controls and policies, typically fulfilled by cyber operations.

 **USE CASE- RMF**: Of the six steps found within RMF, the last step, Monitor is focused on cyber operations, whereas steps 1 through 5 are establishing a baseline of controls, policies and accreditation. To enhance cybersecurity, we must monitor and illustrate the viability and health of the security standards deployed. Unfortunately, many organizations spend 90% of their time on establishing a baseline of controls and 10% of their time on enhancing their cyber posture – achieving cyber accountability.

As we continue to strive to enhance our cybersecurity posture, we must strike a balance between planning and execution. The RMF steps do not represent time allocation per se, although too frequently represent a lack of balance between cyber planning and cyber operational activities.

The following "Cyber Steps" enable organizations to achieve Cyber Accountability. As an example, listed are the **BAP** and RMF Cyber Steps.

BAP Cyber Steps	RMF Cyber Steps
Step 1: Build and discover your cyber needs	Step 1: Categorize the needs to meet DoD cyber needs. Step 2: Design and Implement Cyber Controls Step 3: Implement the cyber controls in the environment
Step 2: Analyze and validate controls and policies	Step 4: Assess the implementation of the cyber controls
Step 3: Protect and provide continuous monitoring of your environment.	Step 6: Provide continuous monitoring of the system

Chapter 2: Step 1: Discover and Build Controls

Step 1 (RMF Steps 1-3): start with a known and established collection of cybersecurity standards. The most significant collection of cyber controls is found within NIST, with the majority in Special Publication NIST 800-53. Regardless of your organization, the collection of standards within NIST is extensive and very impressive. Use the NIST control as a starting point for RMF and modify the controls to meet the requirements of your environment. Equally as important as building a collection of controls, is the management of the controls, the implementation language and the development of policy.

Save time and cost. When building your controls, use the correct tool.

Preinstalled cyber controls and policies within the application. The key to saving time and cost is to develop a set of controls that can be applied to multiple security policies, effortlessly, with a software application like BAP. The objective of the cybersecurity control is a known variable, whereas the implementation of the security control will be modified based on the security policy. Providing consistency within the controls, which for many environments will be hundreds of controls, is essential for all systems (a collection of cyber controls to meet a specific business objective: e-mail, database, files) you wish to secure within your environment. Encryption, for example, is important to multiple systems within your organization, hence the encryption standard will be a constant, whereas the implementation of encryption will vary dependent upon the policy that requires encryption: e-mail and web application.

Validate the accuracy of the implementation language associated with each cyber control and provide a "report card" outlining the strength of the implementation of the security control, typically, before the physical implementation begins.

The ability to share cyber controls and policies with others using the same application, enabling a centralized site to create collections of controls and policies for other sites within their organization. The ability to share controls and policies should be available for connected and disconnected environments and should always be free.

Maximizing time invested to develop the cyber security controls with the addition and correlation to the real-time threat to your environment.

The ability to inherit a single cyber control to multiple cyber policies. Inheritance should allow for a cascade effect when changes occur to your controls in the future, saving you time and cost.

As organizations build their RMF infrastructure they can begin the process by inputting their controls and policies into **BAP**. **BAP** enables RMF control modifications, and the ability to inherit and organize controls into cyber policy. **BAP** software enables RMF policy cyber professionals to transition their efforts easily to cyber operational teams to provide visibility to the viability of the controls and policies created.

Discovery of Cyber Standards

Discovery of cyber objectives is a critical step to any cybersecurity strategy. With **bapReader** and **bapOCS**, organizations can quickly understand and build a list of controls and policies needed within their environment. **bapReader** can review existing policy documents and provide a mapping to NIST controls. **bapOCS** allows customers to select from cybersecurity objectives, leading the customer to develop a custom set of controls and policies.

Gain 50% more visibility out of the box

Following a successful discovery of cyber needs, **BAP Jumpstart** – RMF provides organizations with immediate visibility to approximately 50% of the cyber controls and policies implemented within RMF. Too often the hill to cyber accountability seems insurmountable, and we lose energy trying to complete all the controls and associated tasks for RMF, while the cyber threat continues to increase. With **BAP Jumpstart** – RMF we have preloaded controls, policies, and implementation language, providing immediate / out-of-the-box cyber accountability, accelerating RMF time to adoption. The use of **BAP Jumpstart** allows immediate results while providing the work environment for staff to improve cyber controls over the course of time. Customers download the **BAP Jumpstart** RMF file and get right to work.

When pre-set controls are not enough

Sites can quickly create custom controls and policies from over 2,500 preloaded security controls, which includes all of the NIST 800-53 controls and enhancements or start from scratch to build their controls. It's as easy as **BAP**.

Chapter 3: Step 2: Validate Controls and Policies

Step 2 (RMF Steps 4-5): Validate the implementation language related to the controls before implementing the controls, reducing cyber operations time to adjust existing infrastructure and add new technologies to the environment to meet control needs. The validation criteria can be authored by the cyber policy and cyber operational teams, producing a vetted system security plan (SSP) and a clear path to continuous monitoring and RMF accountability.

USE CASE- RMF: RMF policy cyber professionals enter all controls into the **BAP** software suite, grouping the controls into policies. The cyber operation teams modify the implementation language associated with each control, as well as implement the control within the environment. The RMF policy and cyber operation teams validate the implementation language used for the controls throughout the process. Following successful validation of the implementation language and controls, steps 1 through 5 are satisfied within RMF, while preparing security operations for successful monitoring of the environment, step 6 within RMF. The groundwork must be completed for RMF, why not complete the work within **BAP**, knowing that continuous monitoring and accountability are core attributes of **BAP** software.

Chapter 4: Step 3: Analyze Cyber Health

Step 3 (RMF Step 6): With the ability to leverage BAP software to automate the creation and validation of security controls and policies, the final step is to provide continuous monitoring of the control and policies implemented.

Continuous monitoring and algorithms

Continuous monitoring is often enabled through algorithms looking for known threat patterns, or the analysis of unexpected behavior within the environment. The understanding of threat to the environment is a step in the right direction, although the results must align with existing security standards to provide cyber accountability.

Cyber accountability is the ability to visualize the impact of the cyber threat to specific services or system (email, GOTs database, mission control) within the environment. Some of the attributes of cyber accountability include:

Automation and artificial intelligence to compare a standard to dynamic variables in an environment to ascertain the viability/health of the stated standard

Provide accountability, based on actual events, to the cyber health of an organization

Use of weights, priorities and key phrases to cumulatively ascertain risk level scores related to any standard and the impact on related standards to meet a common objective, cyber risk being a primary outcome

Focused resolution on non-compliant and risk-oriented events

 **USE CASE- RMF**: An agency defines and implements security controls using the RMF guidelines. The agency installs continuous monitoring solutions for the firewalls, networks, and servers. The viability or health of the firewalls, networks, servers is established through policies and in some cases automated remediation. Immediately following an attack, the Commander asks, "What is the impact to the systems that we currently have an ATO"?

USE CASE- RMF: A DoD agency, AVSD (Autonomic Vehicle Safety for DoD-(not an actual Federal Agency)) has 300 different components within their environment (components are hardware or software like network firewalls, operating systems, applications, and databases). Using the RMF Framework, AVSD has implemented 500 individual cyber controls supporting 100 policies.

With 300 different components and 500 controls, what is the cyber risk or impact of an event to the health of the controls? The breached firewall has a direct negative cyber impact on three controls and over 40 other cyber controls ranging from access control to mobility to encryption (see Appendix A for details).

Continuous Monitoring and Accountable Security

Continuous monitoring is the first step; as is the deployment of SIEM, Log Aggregation, and Cyber Operations teams, although to understand the actual threat to the agency, the agency must move beyond SIEM and Log Aggregation into Accountable Cyber.

The use of log aggregators and SIEM products have significantly enhanced our ability to find that needle in the haystack, allowing us to create scripts and algorithms to discover the threat to our environment. Industry recognizes the value in these products, although the effort required, often exceeds that of the traditional IT administrator.

The impact of the firewall breach is not as simple as an exposed port on the firewall; the breach also increases the risk level of other hardware and software within the secured system. Because of the breached firewall, the risk level of multiple components increases, elevating the risk to the components within the AVSD system:

- The AVSD router risk score increased from a two to a seven
- The AVSD network switch risk score increased from a one to a four
- The AVSD LDAP server risk score increased from a two to a five

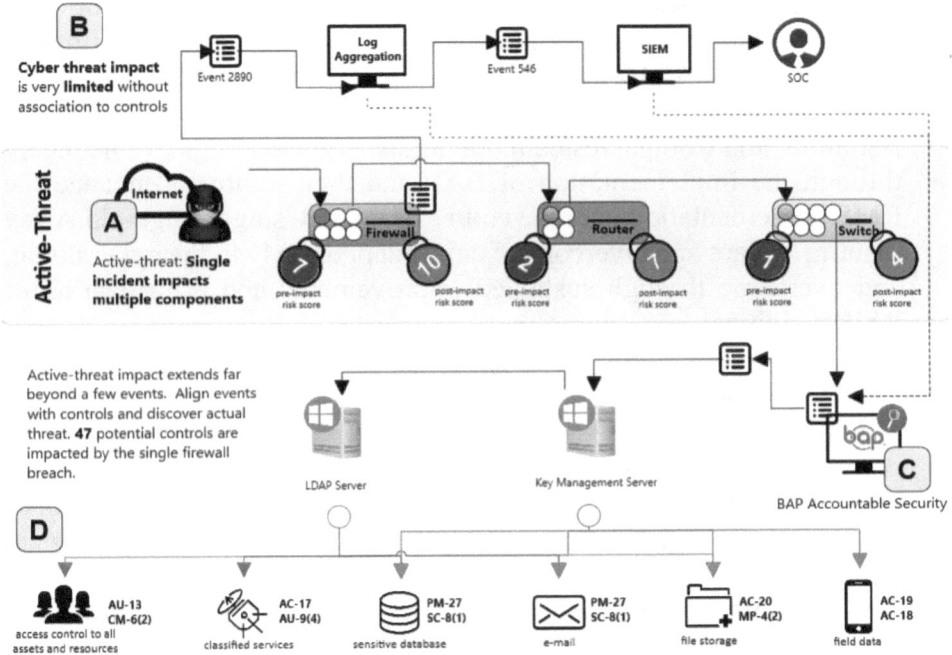

The use of SIEM or log aggregators will reduce the number of events to be processed, although the mathematical algorithms needed to understand the risk level impact is very complicated, based on the staggering potential implications and varying levels of impact, controls, and policies.

Build the RMF standards within **BAP**. Continuous monitoring and Accountable Security are within reach. Continuous monitoring and accountability do not have to be an insurmountable task; BAP makes it easy.

 USE CASE- RMF: The AVSD security operations team, utilizing the BAP software suite, analyzes event information received by the bapAI, providing near real-time visibility of control health. AVSD has visibility as to the cyber health/viability of all security controls and policies implemented throughout AVSD.

The 106th Signal Brigade S3 manages the RMF implementation for the Brigade. The objective is to centrally manage the distribution of standards, built upon NIST 800-53 while following the guidelines of RMF, enabling Alpha and Bravo Companies within the 154th Signal Battalion to move quickly through the six levels of RMF. The Brigade, Battalion, and Companies gain operational cyber strength immediately through the implementation of BAP and then return to enhance the RMF implementation over the course of time. Using the age-old Army mantra, "Adapt and Overcome," units adapt quickly to the cyber threat, and overcome through sustained improvements and prioritization of RMF activities.

Organization accountability is possible

Achieving cybersecurity strength is possible when organizations view the creation of cyber controls and policies as the absolute point of reference from which we measure cyber accountability. The process to implement an RMF environment is involved, although the addition of the BAP software suite allows agencies to optimize time and cost to achieve the goal: a robust cyber defense for our nation and citizens. BAP enables the centralized management of the implementation of RMF providing cost and time-savings, as well as sharing standards throughout the organization.

Providing Accountability

Building an accountable cyber environment requires the correlation between active threat found in event logs to the controls and policies established within RMF. The hardware and software manufacturers define the events, NIST and the local command defines the cyber controls, both of which are known variables. As a result, the analytics engine can predict the health of the cyber implementation with greater accuracy versus looking for anomalies or other complex algorithms. As the event log produces a pre-defined and known error code, the event is aligned with defined security controls, providing true cyber accountability.

Validation

Commands can dictate the frequency at which all of the controls are deployed and reviewed to support RMF. Commands modify the implementation of the controls to meet mission requirements while maintaining validation and oversight as needed. The command can now take full advantage of an accountable cybersecurity environment shortly following the BAP installation. The flexibility of using BAP for RMF provides agencies the ability to meet mission requirements immediately while fine-tuning the cybersecurity strategy as time allows.

Chapter 5: Events and Cyber Accountability

Event logs play an essential role to understand the active threat to the organization, to include sub-organizations. There are many ways to collect events from an environment.

Collecting events from the environment
Log Aggregators and SIEMs: BAP can collect data directly from hardware or as a consolidated log from log aggregators and SIEMS. For large enterprise environments, a log aggregator is used to parse the tens of thousands of events into a more manageable event log before submitting to the bapFramework. BAP accepts logs from many different sources.
Push from hardware: a push of event logs is typically a server-side script or third-party product that runs locally on a hardware platform that collects current event logs and pushes them to a "target" directory, like BAP in a centralized location. Once the logs are in the BAP location, the BAP AI processes the logs.
Pull from hardware: a pull requires that a driver is installed upon the source server, and data is extracted from the source and replicates the data to a "target" directory, like BAP in a centralized location. Once the logs are in the BAP location, the BAP AI processes the logs.
BAP accepts data as a push target. BAP integrates with common replication software applications to move data into BAP for analysis. The BAP framework may also be installed in a "disconnected" environment allowing for patches, updates, and reports using removable media.

Manual feed of events for highly security

The manual update of event logs within BAP enables organizations to leverage BAP as an audit tool. Manual log updates are not a recommended configuration, as manual log updates do not provide continuous monitoring, although may be leveraged as an RMF inspection tool for commands and sub-commands and for highly secure and disconnected environments.

Chapter 6: Cyber Health for Multiple Sites

The phases of RMF are satisfied easily within the BAP framework. The objective is to establish a secure front-line and then to reinforce the front line over the course of time as situational awareness of the cyber threat increases. BAP is explicitly designed to produce immediate results while enabling the constant fine-tuning and improvement of the organization's cyber posture.

All BAP frameworks within the Brigade receives data from the Battalions for reporting, dashboards, and forensics. Fort Polk, Fort Sill, and Fort Hood all participate in a joint training exercise. The training exercise will include red team attacks on each of the Forts. Fort Gordon will monitor the health of the RMF infrastructure for all sites. The centralization of health status does not interfere with the autonomy required at each of the Forts. Data is encrypted and replicated to Fort Gordon enabling centralized analysis for the joint training exercise or specific health status of the participating forts.

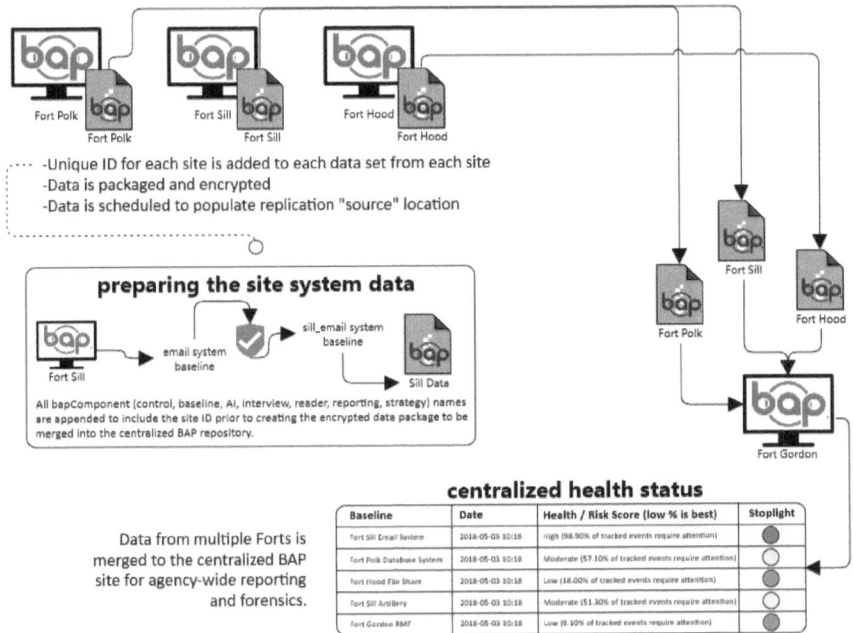

Chapter 7: Remediation – POA&M

As agencies identify and develop plans to address gaps in cyber analytic capabilities and risk management efforts, bapValidate, bapRemediate, and bapAudit can help. To address gaps organizations must first define a baseline that accurately captures their cyber objectives, for example, RMF. Then, using the BAP artificial intelligence and analytics, BAP draws a contrast between the actual state and the desired state.

Prioritization of cyber health is dependent upon our ability to focus on systematic risks that begins with the discovery of events as they impact defined controls and policies. Events discovered within the environment can be quickly prioritized using bapRemediate. bapRemediate provides a POA&M format as well.

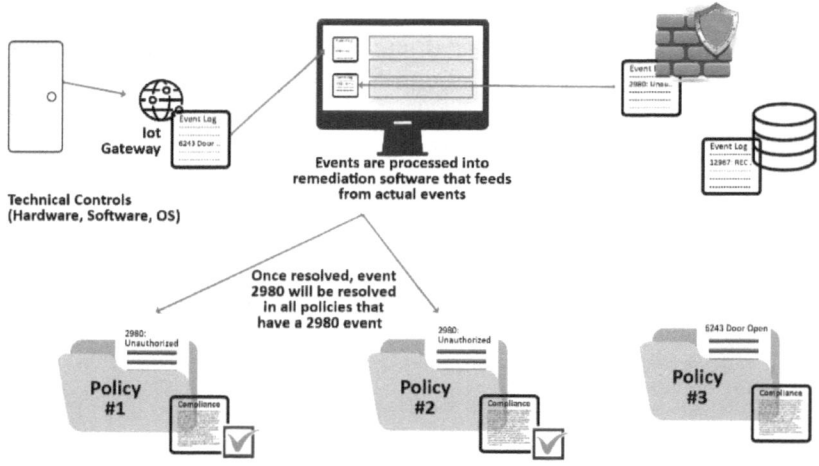

Addressing the most significant risk first and focusing on the highest impact systems, assets and capabilities is a practical approach to cyber remediation. Remediation of risk is dependent upon understanding the direct and indirect impact of the cyber compromise. Once established, remediation efforts must be presented, organized and managed through the application of milestones, budgetary restrictions, third-party dependencies, assignment of resources and suspense dates. bapRemediate allows organizations to align actual threat to their environment against established cyber controls and policies, funneling remediation requirements for immediate action.

Integration of remediation functions, within a control framework, enables organizations to identify and remediate risk quickly. As events are resolved, the event should be fixed for all associated remediation efforts. For example, event 2980 is resolved and updated for Policy #1 and Policy #2.

Chapter 8: The impact of Data Collection

Data collection activities, whether the organization forces regulatory requirements or performance objectives, information must be collected, managed, validated and ultimately become accountable. The information is obtained, which has a cost that includes data collection efforts/staff time, software to collect and organize the data, staff to review/manage the data - once, twice, three times before the information is submitted to meet the compliance need. The quality of the data and time required is a real cost to the organization that is realized in staff utilization and potential penalties as a result of the quality of the data collected.

Data collection activities extend deep within our organizations to include technical and non-technical efforts at an ever-increasing rate, making artificial intelligence and automation a must-have for all organizations.

Compliance is no longer a checkbox exercise. Regulatory compliance in 2018 continues to penalize organizations for noncompliance, with many organizations paying substantial fines and loss of business revenue. To exasperate the challenge, the cyber threat within our society continues to increase, making compliance activities a critical path to success for all organizations.

Building a data collection model

Building a data collection strategy typically requires little investment, merely a reallocation of resources. Many organizations continue to use a data collection strategy based on technologies and process dating back multiple decades.

With the increased data collection demand, now is the time to insert artificial intelligence to assist with your organization and move into the 21st century. Many organizations are making strides toward the future, although without simplified management, validation of our efforts, and continuous monitoring accountability, results are difficult to achieve. BAP software provides a framework to:

1. **Simplify the creation and collection of data** through automated data collection all within a self-contained virtual appliance.

2. **Validation of information** provided by the individual submitting the data, as well as an enterprise view of all data collected.

3. **Continuous monitoring and accountability** of all information received ensuring the organizations best effort for continuous compliance, as well as non-technical reports for stakeholders to monitor their organization.

The collection and management of information both internally and externally is a difficult task, for most organizations there are 2 types of data collection:

- One time or reoccurring collection of information often referred to as "data calls"
- Regulatory collection required for compliance such as PII, PCI…

Efficiencies and cost savings are recognized as organizations leverage technology to assist with the process.

Common tasks for data collection

Multiple device collection. When information is distributed does the recipient have to use specific software to respond? The cost should be calculated for the software required. Convenience is an indirect cost based on the value of the data as it impacts additional cost or revenue streams within the organization.

Distribute/Collect/Manage information in a highly secure and network isolated environment. What is the value of information within sensitive areas?

Immediate User Feedback enables the recipient of the interview to be more accurate in their response, inadvertently lowering cost and increasing collection times.

Enterprise visibility of the data collected. The strength of the information collection is dependent on the ability to see all responses for the enterprise.

Correlate "real-time" events to the information collected, as applicable, continually providing the organization with continuous monitoring. With multiple regulations like GDPR, DFARS, PII and others, event correlation can be very powerful for organizations of all sizes.

1. **Copy / Re-Use** existing data collections. Solutions must provide the ability to copy, edit, delete, clone and use parts of past data collections.

2. **Locate files**. Ability to find data collections quickly in a structure environment.

3. **Build custom data collections** allows 100% flexibility as to the information collected.

4. **Distribute data collections** via social media, text message or email consistently.

5. **Validate and re-certify** the accuracy of the data collected, while providing feedback. For improvement. BAP software enables organizations to extend their current data collection leveraging technology to dramatically reduce cost and increase functionality within any environment, from business to the government.

Cost of data collection to understand the cost of data collection and regulatory certification we need to assign time to each of the common tasks. Understanding this information allows us to get cost comparison to current labor intensive tasks within our organization. We are confident that there is a real cost associated with data collection and that **BAP** can save cost while adding validation and accountability, without increasing your budget spend.

Cost per data collection task	Labor hours for data call	BAP Labor hours for data call
Correlate real-time events to collection	0	0

Copy / re-use data collected from the past	.5	.33
Locate files for the collection	.5	.08
Build custom data collections	4	.75
Validate collected information	10	.5
TOTAL LABOR HOURS	15	2.16
Based on a 72k annual employee salary performing the work, the cost for the data collection	$600	$86.67
BAP Cost savings per data call	.	$513.33

Cost of certification

Cost per certification	Labor hours for certification	BAP Labor hours for certification
Correlate real-time events to collection of certification information	80	.16
Copy / re-use data collected from the past certifications	1	.33
Locate files for the collection	.5	.08
Build custom data collections	8	.5
Validate collected information	125	8

TOTAL LABOR HOURS	214.5	9.08
Based on a 72k annual employee salary performing the work, the cost for the certification	$8,580	$363.33
BAP Cost Savings per certification		$8,216.67

Your numbers may differ from the chart above. Perhaps ask yourself, if I send out a data call to 10 people, how much time will the effort require? We are very conservative and estimate that you will spend at least 15 hours.

Imagine sending multiple data calls, mix in a few certification and re-certification efforts, and you will soon discover the amazing time savings available when using **BAP**. Time savings directly exposes cost savings, although the added functionality of **BAP** will allow your organization to increase the accuracy and effectiveness of your data collection and certification efforts.

With an increased number of certifications and data collection efforts organizations struggle with effective management and accuracy of data collected. BAP enables organizations to work a little smarter without increasing the current budget. A few unique features with BAP include

1. **Multiple device collection.** When information is distributed does the recipient have to use specific software to respond? Convenience to answer your data collection will have a direct correlation with the success of your effort. Make is easier for the recipient and you will increase your data collection.

2. **Distribute/Collect/Manage** information should be consistent and intuitive. For annual certification image updating the information quickly over the course of the year. Do not spend time trying to remember where everything is located, BAP can help.

3. **Immediate User Feedback** enables the recipient of the interview to be more accurate in their response, inadvertently lowering cost and increasing collection times. Proving immediate feedback and suggested correction strengthens your data collection and compliance efforts, progressively getting better every year.

4. **Enterprise visibility** of the data collected. The strength of the information collection is dependent on the ability to see all responses for the enterprise. Enterprise management, distribution, comparisons, dashboards and reporting should be the default for any data collection effort, and with BAP it is a default feature.

Chapter 9: Validation and Accountability

Validation

If the data collection has not been validated for accuracy, the data may create an increased workload that may cause the data to never be fully utilized. BAP provides validation in several ways:

As the recipient of the data collection request they complete their input and are provided with instant scoring of their content. The BAP Artificial Intelligence uses a series of key phrases (customizable by the originator of the data collection request) and searches the provided content. If the key phrase is not found, the recipient is given hints and allowed to modify their submission. The result: The originator receives accurate input and the recipient receives training on expectations related to the data collection, a real win-win.

Validation scores are collected by all the data collection requests and forwarded to the enterprise for an enterprise view of the data collection.

Accountability

Beyond validation of the data collection, BAP enables continuous monitoring of the questions within the collected data that have electronic tracked events. BAP provides customers with the following for accountability:

Use BAP to create custom control and correlate events within the environment to provide continuous monitoring of the control health.

Often data collection and certification is a hybrid effort between technical and non-technical data. The BAP framework provides the ability to link all data together for enterprise health.

The line between data collection and certification and cyber accountability continues to blur. BAP integrates cyber with your data collection and certification efforts, providing a library of over 4,000 controls and several tools.

Chapter 10: The "real" cost of Cyber

Chapter 10 will address the following:

- **One**: Can I make my existing cyber tools meet fluid cyber threat and requirements? Are our cyber investments aligned to support our cyber objectives and policies?

- **Two**: Does my cyber visualization tell me how secure I am, or does it produce data that is confusing and difficult to understand?

- **Three:** Cyber cost is more than a component or piece of software. Do I understand all the variables that contribute to cyber cost?

Calculate cost for cyber environments

The following pages breakdown all potential costs associated with maintaining a cyber environment, although individual situations will differ considerably, the following should provide direction and guidance on understanding your cyber cost. The analysis compares cyber software costs that include hardware, software, the configuration of controls and their implementation, management of a security operations center, and remediation preparation for events that have occurred.

BAP provides levels of automation that have a direct impact on driving down cost related to building and managing a cyberinfrastructure.

Some cost savings are more specific to making a cyber structure, although even these environments have maintenance costs that will recognize cost savings through cyber automation.

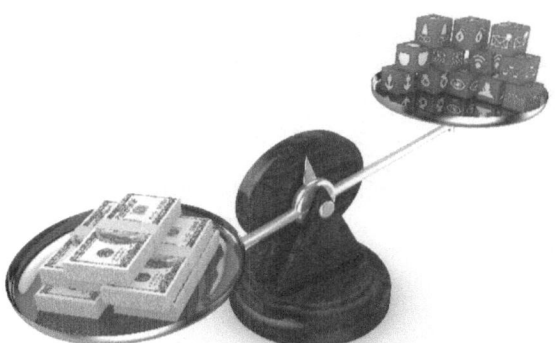

Will BAP replace existing tools?

BAP will replace some of the tools in your environment, although others will work nicely to enhance the functionality of BAP and provide you with a comfort level of using legacy tools.

We will explore questions and thoughts about evaluating cyber cost within our environments. Often, cyberinfrastructure is implemented to meet regulatory and compliance requirements, with the ultimate objective to protect the environment and assets within the environment. BAP provides accountability through the alignment of events to your security standards.

Summary of cyber cost impact and savings

Included below are for summary statements representing the cost models defined on the following pages. Your results will differ, as there are too many variables to take into consideration when building cost models, although as you read the following pages, you will discover there are substantial cost savings available for your organization when implementing BAP.

CYBER INVESTMENTS: Starting with the core infrastructure, BAP reduces server hardware, operating system, and storage costs, while providing automation to establish security controls and policies, coupled with maintenance accountability accelerating time to remediation. See the details on following pages and see how your environment may save up to $500,000.

SOC ANALYSTS: Security operation centers are staffed to address the real-time threat. Within an environment that operates 24 hours a day, seven days a week and 365 days a year with a staff of four per shift, BAP can deliver an estimated $1.7 million in cost savings annually through pinpointed alignment of the threat to specific security controls, reducing the number of required analysts.

MANAGING THREAT: The average cost for processing events that occur daily within the environment involves investigation and remediation management. Cost includes investigation time to narrow down the point of impact and the tracking and management of remediation. As an example, if seven events occurred within the environment in a 24-hour period, and it takes 90 minutes to investigate (total FTE time), and 30 minutes to document and prepare for remediation activities, BAP will potentially save the organization $500,692.

NON-COMPLIANCE FINANCIAL IMPACT: Noncompliance with cyber regulations will continue to have a negative revenue impact for organizations that do not enhance their cyber health and compliance. As an example, if your annual revenue is $1 million with 30% of your business from the EU and 10% of your business from the US Department of Defense, and you are found to be noncompliant, the first-year revenue impact could result in losses of 52% or $515,000. Year two is a little better with the loss of approximately $400,000.

Do existing Cyber Tools support my Controls? Can I make my existing cyber tools meet fluid cyber threat and requirements?

It seems like just yesterday that adding cyber protection to an information technology environment was an afterthought, an extra cost. Move the clock forward a few decades, and cyber security should be the first thought when designing or managing an information technology environment. Many of our environments leverage cyber technologies and strategies that are decades old. How do I know if my existing cyber tools? We  continue to evaluate risk based on components found within the environment (i.e., firewalls LDAP servers, etc.). Perhaps we do not realize that cyber risk presents itself as a threat against the "collection of all components" within our environments, or what is referred to as a "system."

Do my cyber tools support my Cyber Strategy?

All cyber tools should support your cyber standards, policies, and strategy. If the cyber tool does not enable your cyber standards, a closer evaluation is in order. If you're looking to make a positive impact on your budget, evaluating the cyber tools against your cyber standards is a productive use of time and resources.

Are your cyber standards and policies more of a paper exercise?

BAP provides over 2,500 cyber standards and policies free with the installation of the BAP virtual appliance. The BAP jumpstart tool allows organizations to quickly establish cybersecurity standards with immediate visibility of active cyber threat.

Can I see how secure I am, right now?

Information technology software is infamous for providing beautiful dashboards and reports of what the future holds for an organization. Although, like many software applications, organizations find the hill of education and integration too steep, and often settle for less than 15% of the software's designed functionality. For many cybersecurity software applications, like log aggregators or SIEM products, there is no doubt that the applications are rich in functionality and value. Is the value helping an organization genuinely understand their cyber health? Many organizations find the steep hills of education and integration for cyber continuous monitoring too steep. Produce results in less than and hour with bapJumpStart.

The implementation and management of many cybersecurity software applications are demanding and expensive. Implementation times can vary from months to years, too often producing cryptic results that fail to align real-time threat with the cyber standards implemented within the environment.

BAP can leverage the output from log aggregators and SIEM solutions to align events to the cyber standards implemented within an organization. BAP can also function independently to ingest logs natively if needed for smaller organizations or remote sites. BAP's unique accountable cyber solution aligns real-time threat with cyber standards within the environment, telling consumers how healthy their cyber standards are.

Cyber cost is more than a single component

Evaluating the cyber health of an environment based on the independent evaluation of components (i.e., firewall, server, network) within the environment is a common practice for many organizations. This form of evaluation has merit, although in today's fluid and volatile cyber environment, as of 2018, component-based cyber health is just scratching the surface.

Cybersecurity threat must be assessed based on system risk, not component-based risk. Like the adverse impact of not carrying a spare when you get a flat. It is not just the tire that is impacted, the entire functionality of vehicle (or the system) that is at risk/non-functional until the component (the tire) is fixed.

What is a component? A component is a piece of hardware, software, person or process designed to support a specific business outcome. For example: to provide an email service (business outcome or system) I must have a firewall, network, operating systems, storage, servers, software, established processes for dealing with operational details, and varied levels of staff.

Understanding the cyber threat or health of a specific component within the system is a good first step. Unfortunately, each component does not act independently in support of the business objective, or system. Contrary, all of the components have a direct and indirect impact on the cyber threat or health of the business objective. This approach to cybersecurity is often referred to as component-based cybersecurity.

Component-based cybersecurity is a lot like evaluating the safety of your vehicle based upon the functionality of your spare tire. The spare tire is minimal, if any risk to the operation of the vehicle, although when combined with multiple events, can present a substantial risk to your health. It's late one evening during a snow storm:

- You do not have a spare tire
- Your cell phone has run out of power
- You realize you have no way of finding the necessary tools to escape the bitter cold; you are in trouble.

Cybersecurity efforts for our information technology environments are like the functionality of our spare tire. Component-based cybersecurity would have only revealed our lack of tire chains, which would have been given a low to insignificant risk level. As the traveler, the inability to arrive at our destination may result in frostbite, hyperthermia or death; the lack of a spare tire as part of the vehicle "system" now presents a considerable risk. Cybersecurity efforts must be calculated based upon system risk and not a component-based risk.

Establish system-based risk with alignment to defined cyber standards for an accurate perspective of your cyber health

With component risk levels established, even when combined as system risk levels, if the risk is not aligned to security standards and policies designed to protect business outcomes, organizations will struggle to understand how secure they are.

BAP provides accountable security. Uniquely, BAP aligns current threat in a real-time methodology and aligns discovered threat with known cyber standards and policies.

Understanding cyber cost is dependent upon existing cyber tool cost, fluid cyber threat, visualization requirements, and component-based methodology for cybersecurity; all of which have direct and indirect costs. Following are a few ideas to get a better understanding of your direct cyber cost.

Infrastructure Cost

Implementing tools in a legacy environment. The figures below reflect a new installation of a specific or set of cyber tools. Adjust the cost of the line items to ascertain your actual cost. Calculating cost based on existing hardware and software is a difficult task as there are many variables to consider. When is the next refresh for the hardware and software? Are cyber tools sharing hardware and software resources or are do the cyber tools require isolated hardware and software? What type of operating system is needed? Do you have to upgrade from a "standard server" to an "enterprise server"? and the list goes on.

The following information is designed to spark your personal creativity in understanding your cost, your actual cost. I can almost guarantee you that your cost is probably higher than you want top know and with BAP it does not have to be.

How does BAP reduce the cost?

BAP was designed specifically to save operational and capital expense. BAP does not require a specific operating system, only a free hypervisor. BAP is 100% self-contained, meaning that BAP has no software dependencies (like a database or specific operating system) and will run on minimal hardware.

Existing / Shared Infrastructure – Sunk Cost?

The cyber tools in your environment are part of a shared or existing infrastructure. For these environments, it can be challenging to define hardware cost. Estimate the total value of the hardware resource and take a percentage of the price to support the cyber tool(s). Bringing you closer to a cost model.

Maintenance and Life Cycle Depreciation.

We can never underestimate the cost of maintenance for hardware that typically has the consumer pay for the software every four years (based on a 15% maintenance fee). Although the hardware cost for today may be a sunk cost, the time will come that the value of the hardware will play a role in the cost of the cyber environment.

Consistency and Repeatability

The following pages will illustrate examples of cost savings with BAP. Every environment will be different. Please use the information provided in the tables, insert your current information and define cost that makes sense for your environment. The reality is that cost savings is available. To drive out cost from information technology practices, to include cyber strategy, environments must introduce consistency and repeatability. Consistency and repeatability will drive down immediate cost and provide the foundation to drive down cost for many years to follow.

Hardware to support existing cyber tools	Current	BAP	Savings with BAP
Cost for the server/desktop that is hosting the cyber tool	$18,000	$2,500	$15,500
The number of servers needed to support the cyber tools	3	1	
Cost of other servers (i.e. virtualization, database, key management) that are required to support the cyber tools	$20,000	$0.00	$20,000
Cost of hardware and storage to support the cyber tools	$12,000	$0.00	$12,000
Sub-total hardware cost	$86,000	$2,500	$83,500
Annual maintenance and support cost (based on 15% annual)	$12,900	$0	$12,900
Total cost	$98,900	$2,500	

One-time savings with BAP – Capital Expense	$83,500
3-year operating expense savings with BAP	$38,700
Total budget savings with BAP	$122,200

Software Cost

Enterprise Agreements

Software licensing in larger environments may be part of an enterprise agreement. Hence the cost may be pushed to another group within the organization. The cost of the software should be considered when evaluating the total cost of a cyber tool.

Cyber Tools as Virtual Appliances

Some cyber tools, like BAP, are delivered as virtual appliances. A virtual appliance can be very favorable from a licensing perspective as frequently as all the required software is contained within the virtual appliance. Pay close attention to the virtual appliance and the related cost. For example, BAP is a virtual appliance that runs in a hypervisor from the free hypervisor version to an enterprise hypervisor. With BAP all software is self-contained within the virtual appliance, requiring no additional software.

What are the software dependencies for the cyber tools? What operating system is required to run the cyber software? Does the cyber software need a database, a specific operating system, perhaps the cyber software requires an enterprise-level version of the server operating system? What are the other cyber software dependencies? What are the costs associated with all dependencies to support the cyber software? What is the reoccurring annual cost for maintenance and support of the software products?

Hardware to support existing cyber tools	Current	BAP	Savings with BAP
Cost of the server(s) operating system to support the cyber tools	$10,000	$0	$15,500
The number of servers needed to support the cyber tools	3	1	$30,000

Cost of database server to support the cyber tools	$28,000	$0.00	$28,000
Cost of other software to support the cyber tool?	$5,000	$0.00	$5,000
Cost of virtualization software to support the cyber tool	$15,000	$0.00	$15,000
Cost of high availability software to support the cyber tool or other software (database, key management)	$9,000	$0	$9,000
Cost of all cyber tools used within the environment that BAP may be able to replace, to include maintenance cost	$100,000	$0	$100,000
BAP cost is directly related to the number of controls. The price will be based on 263 controls (FISMA Moderate) and is an annual cost	$0	$78,000	$<78,000>
Maintenance cost for year 2 and year 3 (based at 15% annual cost)	$50,100	$156,000	$<106,000>
Total budget savings with BAP		$18,500	

Preparing the Environment

What preparatory software needs to be installed before the installation of the cyber software? For example, the cyber software requires a specific operating system version or a database to be installed. Make a note of the time needed for the installation as well as the skill set required. Does this expertise exist within your organization or will this be a services engagement with a third-party? Historically, installation services are a short-term engagement ranging from one week to multiple months. What is the cost to install the preparatory software so that the cyber software will run correctly?

Virtualization Software

Virtualization software may include, for example, VMWare or Microsoft. Does the cyber software tool require virtualization software? What level of virtualization software can be used? Can the cyber software run on a free version of virtualization software? What is the cost of the virtualization software?

In many environments, a virtual infrastructure may already be in place. To calculate the cost, you must understand the cost of each virtual machine. The cost of a virtual machine is typically based on the amount of "virtual RAM, virtual CPU cores and virtual disk" used to support the cyber tool. Each of the virtual machines has an associated cost.

Redundancy

Does the cyber software tool require a redundant system? What is the cost of the redundant system as well as the high availability software for the cyber software or the cyber software's dependent software?

Installation Services

How long does it take to install the cyber software? Remember that the time to install the cyber software differs from the time to configure the software. Make a note of the time required for the installation as well as the labor skill level demanded. Does this labor expertise exist within your organization or will this be a services engagement with a third-party? If contracting with a third party, be aware of the length of this engagement and associated cost. Historically, installation services are a short-term engagement ranging from one week to multiple months. What is the cost to install the cyber software?

Installation Services	Current	BAP	Savings with BAP
Using an (2) internal resource, how many hours will be required for the resources to install all cyber tools? Time should include installation of hardware and software.	180	1	179 hours of labor
What is the hourly cost of the internal resource? (i.e.: $150,000/yr. is $87/hr. when considering hours and 20% burden cost)	$87.00	$87.00	
Total Cost	$13,920	$87.00	$13,833

Configuration Services

The configuration of the software is interpreted as the cyber software becoming functional within the environment. Make a note of the time required for the initial setup, as well as the skill set needed.

How much time is required for the continual optimization of the configuration? Does this expertise exist within your organization or will there be a services engagement with a third-party to complete the effort? Historically, configuration services can quickly become a staff augmentation exercise with long-term service engagements. What is the cost to configure the cyber software?

Frequently configuration and installation services are thought of as the same cost, although with Cyber, the installation of the cyber tool is the integration and connection with dependent software, whereas the configuration of the cyber software tool may take an extended period as the tool learns about the threat and the uniqueness of the environment. Configuration services are limited to the software and do not include the development of the cyber controls.

Configuration Services	Current	BAP	Savings with BAP
Using an (2) internal resource, how many hours will be required for the	320	10	310 hours of labor

resources to configure all cyber tools?			
What is the hourly cost of the internal resource? (i.e.: $150,000/yr. is $87/hr. when considering hours and 20% burden cost)	$87.00	$87.00	
Total Cost	$27,840	$870.00	$26,970

Control Development Services

What is the time required to develop your cyber standards, often referred to as cyber controls? In many organizations, the development of standards is completed by the risk management and compliance teams.

Configuration Services	Current	BAP	Savings with BAP
Using an (2) internal resource, how many hours will be required for the resources to customize the controls, group into policies, etc. (i.e. 2 controls per hour, with 263 controls we will need 131 hours. BAP automates much of the process)	262	50	81 hours of labor
What is the hourly cost of the internal resource? (i.e.: $150,000/yr. is $87/hr. when considering hours and 20% burden cost)	$116.00	$116.00	
Total Cost	$30,392	$5,800	$24,592

The development of your cyber standards *does not include the implementation of the cyber standards*, only the development of the standards into policy. For some environments, this may include a fresh start to develop the cyber standards whereas others may be modifying existing cyber standards. The development of your cyber standards will include the adjustment of the implementation language. The development of your cyber standards should reveal the utilization of your existing cyber software. In most cases, if you are utilizing cyber software that does not support your cyber standards, careful consideration as to the value of this cyber software should be evaluated.

Risk Management and SOC

Risk management of the cyberinfrastructure often includes a security operation center (SOC). Is your security operation center managed internally or are you leveraging a contracted service? If your security operation center is managed internally, you need to calculate the cost for the security operation center space, power, hardware, software, and staff. If your security operation center is a contracted service, you need to include the cost of that service as well.

Risk Management (Cyber Operations, SOC)	Current	BAP	Savings with BAP
Using internal SOC resources, how many resources are used in SOC operations?	20	12	Re-allocate 8 of 20 SOC staff
What is the hourly cost of the internal resource? (i.e.: $150,000/yr. is $87/hr. when considering hours and 20% burden cost)	$102.00	$102.00	
What is the one-time standup cost for power, hardware, software and	$20,000	$10.000	$10,000

space to support the SOC?			
Total labor cost to support the SOC	$4,204,400	$2,416,381.15	$1,788,018.85

Cyber Health of your Controls?

Is your security operation center providing you with the cyber health of your controls or are they remediating and preventing known threat without correlation to the health of the security standards implemented? Most security operation centers use technology to discover and deter known threat to the environment, assessment of risk priority and remediation. What is the cost for your security operations? For some situations, this may be the calculation of the help desk staff member or a fractional cost of an individual performing multiple tasks.

Remediation

As a threat occurs, the SOC analysts investigate the event to remediate as soon as possible. The investigation includes understanding the threat. BAP enhances the analyst's ability to understand threat through direct alignment of risk to events in the environment.

Remediation of the event

Remediation is the ability to resolve the event. BAP provides automation to track events, based on actual events in the environment. Time and cost savings are recognized with the automation and management of the events.

Risk Management (Cyber Operations, SOC)	Current	BAP	Savings with BAP
How many security threats are received per day?	7		BAP provides an AI to ascertain security threat
What is the average time, in minutes to investigate the threat?	90	60	30 minutes saved per threat
What is the average time, in minutes to prepare the remediation paperwork?	30	15	15 minutes saved per threat
What is the hourly cost of the internal resource? (i.e.: $150,000/yr. is $87/hr. when considering hours and 20% burden cost)	$116	$116	
Number of hours per month (based on 30 days per month) to resolve and document threat	420	262.5	157.5
Monthly cost to investigate and complete the remediation tasks and paperwork (based on a 30 day month of 210 threats per month)	$48,720	$30,450	$18,270

Appendix A: Firewall Breach

The firewall breach has a ripple effect on multiple components within the system, as well as controls you selected for Cyber. Each control within Cyber has a different risk score based on weights and priorities, calculations that exceed the functionality of SIEM and Log Aggregation. Cyber Accountability is the complete view of the system (hardware, software in your environment) that includes understanding all the risks, cumulatively for all impacted components.

BAP uniquely analyzes the impact to all the controls in the policy to provide an accurate representation of the health of your Cyber controls and policies. **BAP** provides Accountable Security. Please contact info@bapsolution.com for more information.

Appendix A provides potential controls that may be impacted by the firewall breach. The list is dependent upon your environment.

Access Control, Controls

The following represent the access control, controls that may be impacted by the breach. All of which impact the environment at different levels.

Control	Security Objective	Potential impact to the environment
AC-2 (6)	Account management-dynamic privilege management	Modification of the account privilege management will have a cascade impact on all systems
AC-2 (7)	Account management-rule-based schemes	Modification of the account privilege management will have a cascade impact on all systems
AC-3	Access enforcement	Modification of the account privilege management will have a cascade impact on all systems
AC-3 (3)	Access enforcement-mandatory access control	Modification of the account privilege management will have a cascade impact on all systems
AC-3 (4)	Access enforcement-discretionary access control	Modification of the account privilege management will have a cascade impact on all systems
AC-3 (5)	Access enforcement-security relevant information	The access control system risk or increases because of the firewall penetration. Modification to the rules established may play sensitive, relevant security information at risk

AC-3 (7)	Access enforcement-role-based access control	Modification of the account privilege management will have a cascade impact on all systems
AC-3 (8)	Access enforcement-revocation of access authorizations	Unauthorized access to the revocation/authorization objectives for the organization can create unwanted and unknown access to sensitive information
AC-3 (10)	access enforcement-audited override of access control mechanisms	change to the audit logging and the environment will be difficult to know who is doing what on the system
AC-4 (15)	information flow enforcement-detection of unsanctioned information	altering the parameters because of unauthorized access will disable desired information flow enforcement
AC-17	remote access	unauthorized users may be granted remote access to the system
AC-18	wireless access	modification to the wireless security can find rogue devices within the system
AC-19	access control for mobile devices	with the growing amount of data on mobile devices unauthorized access may create a substantial impact
AC-20	use of external information systems	modifications to controls for rent external information systems may lead to loss of sensitive data

Audit, Configuration, Identity and Maintenance Controls

The following represent the controls from audit, configuration, identity and maintenance control families that may be impacted by the breach. All of which impact the environment at different levels.

Control	Security Objective	Potential impact to the environment
AU-9 (4)	Protection of audit information-access by subset of privileged users	Change the audit logging in the environment will be difficult to know who is doing what on the system
AU-13	Monitoring for information disclosure	Monitoring can be disabled when a threat is present
CM-6 (2)	Configuration settings-respond to unauthorized changes	Safeguards can be modified by unauthorized users because of the security breach
CM-7 (4)	Least functionality-unauthorized software and blacklisting	Unauthorized software application list is modified to allow harmful applications in the environment
CM-8 (3)	Information system component inventory-automated unauthorized component detection	Component inventory can be modified to include harmful components to the environment
IA-2 (12)	Identification and authentication (organizational users)-acceptance of PIV credentials	PIV credentials can be modified by unauthorized individual
IA-12	Identity proofing	User identity information can be falsely modified
IR-4	Incident handling	Harmful incidents can be silenced and ignored

		creating risk to the environment
MA-5 (1)	Maintenance personnel-individuals without appropriate access	Personnel security clearances can be modified by unauthorized access
MA-5 (2)	Maintenance personnel-security clearances for classified systems	Access to classified systems can be granted to unauthorized individuals
MP-2	Media access	Rogue media restrictions and safeguards can be disabled
MP-4 (2)	Media storage-automated restricted access	Access to media storage areas can be granted by unauthorized individuals

Physical Access, Program Management, Risk Assessment, System and Communication Protection Controls

The following represent the controls from Physical Access, Program Management, Risk Assessment, System and Communication Protection control families that may be impacted by the breach. All of which impact the environment at different levels.

Control	Security Objective	Potential impact to the environment
PE-2	Physical access authorizations	Contractors and employees can be given physical access without proper authorization
PE-2 (1)	Physical access authorizations-access by position and role	Positions and rolls can be modified to allow for unauthorized access
PE-3	Physical access control	Physical access authentication, verification

		audit logs can be modified without proper authority
PE-3 (1)	Physical access control-information system access	Physical access authorization to facility and systems can be modified by unauthorized individual
PE-5	Access control for output devices	Unauthorized individuals can be given access to obtain sensitive information output
PE-8	Visitor access records	Visitor record logs can be changed by unauthorized individual
PM-27	Individual access control	Privacy act system of records checkpoints can be altered by unauthorized individuals
PS-6 (2)	Access agreements-classified information requiring special protection	Access to classified information can be modified by unauthorized individual
RA-5 (5)	Vulnerability scanning-privileged access	Vulnerability scanning result can be modified and present risk
SC-4	Information in shared resource	Information sharing access can be modified by unauthorized individual
SC-5 (1)	Denial of service protection-restricted internal users	Provide the ability for individuals to launch denial of service attacks against other systems

Appendix B: VA OIG Report

The following information represents an analysis of the OIG FISMA Compliance Report for the US Department of Veterans Affairs (VA) that is available to the public. The VA is the world's largest civilian agency, hence change and improvements can present a substantial challenge. BAP is designed to assist and address many of the issues and challenges the VA is experiencing and is very applicable to many large organizations throughout the globe.

The review process gathers related lexicon/phrases throughout the report and groups the information into specific categories, as seen in the pie chart below. As individuals we use multiple phrases to communicate, for example: Remediation is a primary concern discussed within the report and the analysis aligns the following "remediation" lexicon: Reconstructing security events, remediation of vulnerabilities, remediation of security weaknesses, security deficiencies, plans of actions and milestones, and POA&Ms.

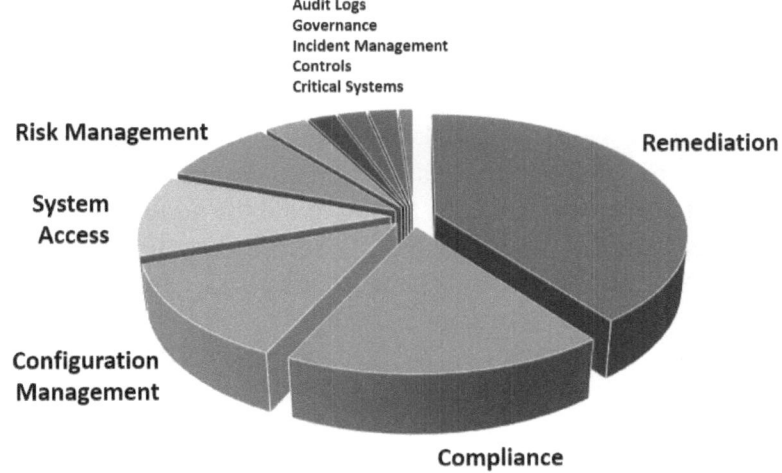

Audit Logging and Monitoring:

"Audit log collections and reviews are critical for evaluating security-related activities, such as determining individual accountability, reconstructing security events, detecting intruders, and identifying system performance issues. Moreover, we have identified and reported deficiencies with audit logging for more than 10 years in our annual FISMA reports."

Unsecured Applications:

"VA has not implemented effective controls to identify and remediate security weaknesses on its web applications."

Baseline Security Configurations:

"We recommended the Executive in Charge for Information and Technology implement more effective automated mechanisms to continuously identify and remediate security deficiencies on VA's network infrastructure, database platforms, and web application servers. (This is a repeat recommendation from prior years.)"

Key Area of Focus

"Address security-related issues that contributed to the information technology material weakness reported in the FY 2017 audit… but much work remains to remediate the significant number of outstanding security weaknesses. POA&Ms identify which actions must be taken to remediate system security risks and improve VA's overall information security posture…. the Department had approximately 8,500 open POA&Ms in FY 2017 as compared with 7,200 open POA&Ms in FY 2016.

How can BAP help?

BAP provides a complete framework to assist organizations to meet their cyber requirements. BAP protects the "system" from the building of the control framework, to analyzing and validating the accuracy of the controls implemented, to protecting the environment through continuously monitoring active threat to the established controls. When an event is discovered, BAP completes the cycle by automating remediation tasks. BAP has a three-step process that includes:

- Build a control framework
- Analyze the health of the controls and polices
- Protect the environment through integrated remediation

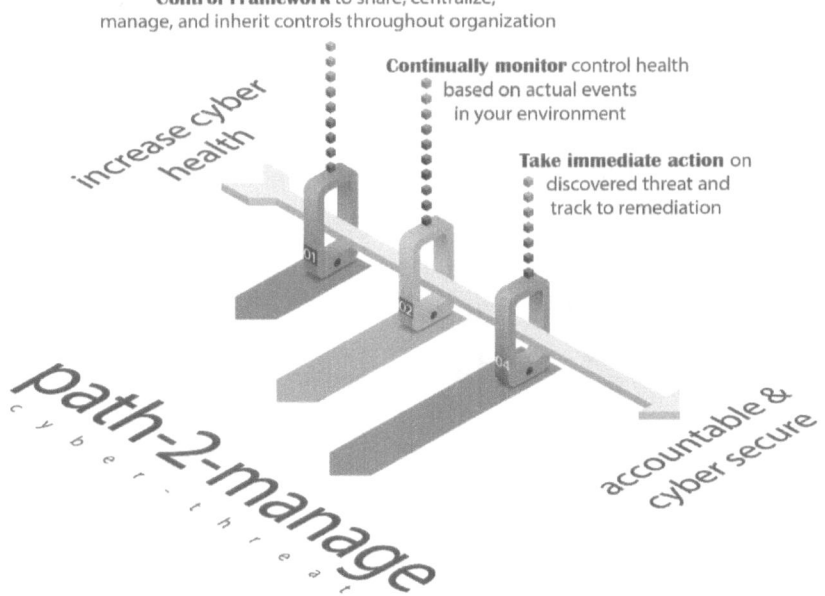

bapEnterprise is a virtual appliance that creates a consistent and repeatable control framework. Like a GRC tool (Governance, Risk and Compliance), BAP takes a control framework to a level unseen in the marketplace. The control framework is the first step for any organization.

For additional VA OIG report details simply search for VA OIG 17-01257-136 on the Internet. We have highlighted a few sections of the OIG report and how BAP can assist, as a real-world use case. The following several pages review the challenge found in the VA and how BAP can help.

Challenge 1 within the VA

- "Audit log deficiencies."
- "Controls to identify and remediate security weaknesses."
- "Implement more effective automated mechanisms to continuously identify and remediate security deficiencies."

The example illustrated in drawing 1 below represents multiple sites sharing log information to ascertain cyber health at each facility, as well as for the enterprise within the VA.

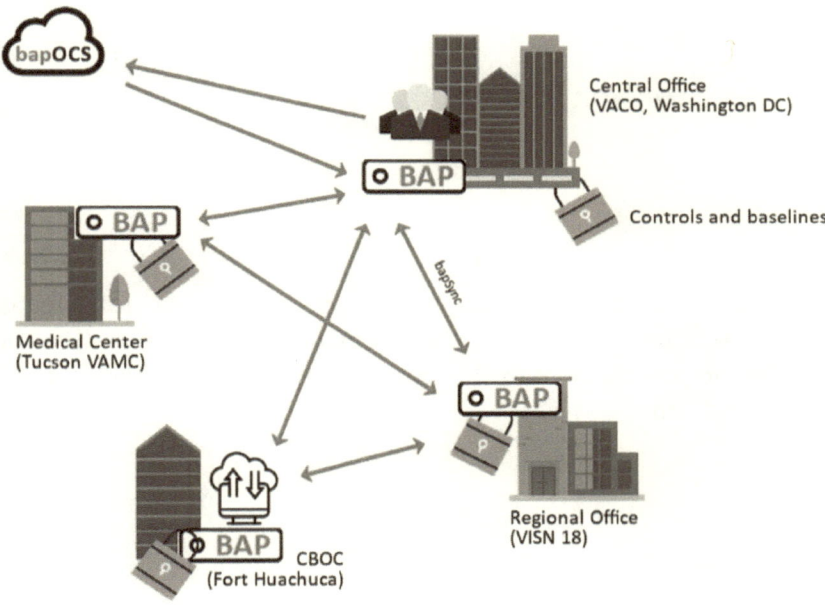

drawing 1

BAP can help with Challenge 1 (see screen shot 1 and 2):
- Virtual appliance installs in minutes, self-contained
- Site functional in less than 2 hours

Example of BAP OCS assisting the VA to build controls consistently within minutes. bapSolution.com/OCS

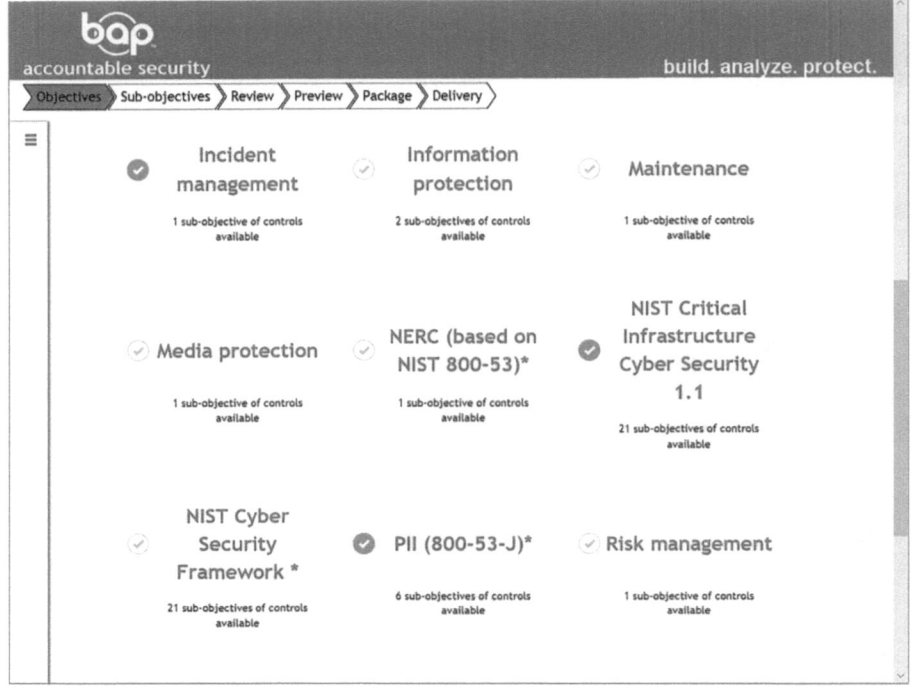

Maintain, manage, create, clone, inherit are a few features available within the control management section of BAP. 100% flexibility to manage control information within the BAP control management tool.

	Objective name	Sub-objective name	Control name	Control description	Preview
☐	NIST Critical Infrastructure Cyber Security 1.1	RS.CO	RS.CO-4 (CSF)	Coordination with stakeholders occurs consistent with response plans	
☐	NIST Critical Infrastructure Cyber Security 1.1	RS.CO	RS.CO-5 (CSF)	Voluntary information sharing occurs with external stakeholders to achieve broader cybersecurity sit	
☐	NIST Critical Infrastructure Cyber Security 1.1	RS.IM	RS.IM-1 (CSF)	Response plans incorporate lessons learned	
☐	NIST Critical Infrastructure Cyber Security 1.1	RS.IM	RS.IM-2 (CSF)	Response strategies are updated	
☐	NIST Critical Infrastructure Cyber Security 1.1	RS.MI	RS.MI-1 (CSF)	Incidents are contained	
☐	NIST Critical Infrastructure Cyber Security 1.1	RS.MI	RS.MI-2 (CSF)	Incidents are mitigated	
☐	NIST Critical Infrastructure Cyber Security 1.1	RS.MI	RS.MI-3 (CSF)	Newly identified vulnerabilities are mitigated or documented as accepted risks	
☐	PII (800-53-J)*	access control	AR-7	Least access privilege for individuals through the development of privacy controls. (NIST 800-53: A	
☐	PII (800-53-J)*	access control	DI-2	Establishes process and accountability for the integrity of PII data through the use of security con	
☐	PII (800-53-J)*	access control	DI-2(1)	Publish of computer matching agreements on the organization's public website. (NIST 800-53: SC-8, SC	

screenshot 2

Challenge 2 within the VA:

- "VA lacks a comprehensive continuous monitoring program to manage information security risks and operations across the enterprise."
- "We continued to identify significant deficiencies in configuration management controls."

BAP can help with Challenge 2:

- Continuous Monitoring by default with event-control mapping.
- API supports Splunk

Building upon a set of controls as the foundation, BAP can maximize the investment by the VA to build complex controls, policies and Splunk rules and jobs and move directly to continuous monitoring to establish the viability and awareness of the effectiveness of meeting challenge 2.

Illustrated in drawing 2, events can be collected directly to BAP servers, for example at Fort Huachuca where there is a smaller collection of hardware and software, to the collection of events at the Tucson VAMC where events are aggregated using Splunk.

All of the events, from both the CBOC and the VAMC can be consolidated and visualized at the VISN office in Gilbert Arizona.

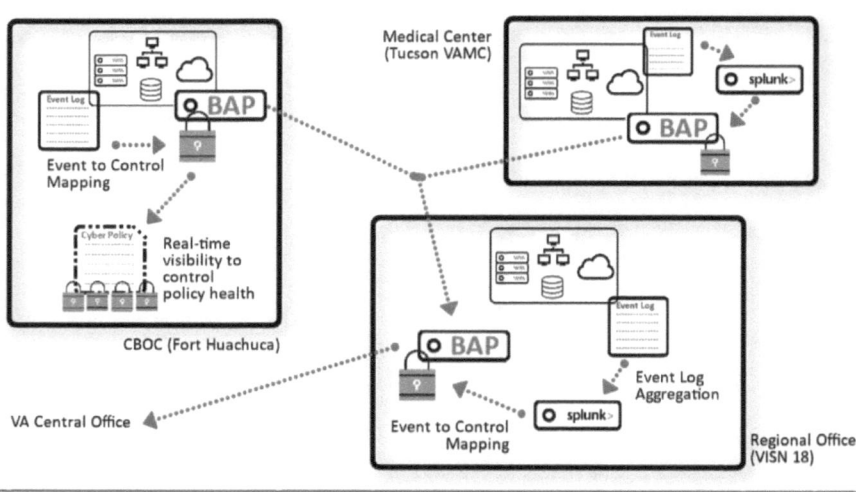

Using the Control Framework as a foundation

The Department of Veterans Affairs is already investing funds to build, organize and implement controls and policies throughout the organization. The addition of BAP can augment that process considerably, and following the development of the controls and policies, can immediately begin continuous monitoring to discover deficiencies in all types of controls running throughout the Department of Veterans Affairs. With time, effort and funds allocated to complete the development of controls and policies, the added benefit of BAP automating and validating the controls and policies, coupled with continuous monitoring of the effectiveness of the controls and policies will most likely save the VA money, with a BAP ROI at less than a year.

The bap Stoplight report (see screenshot 3) provides and easy to understand status on the health of compliance and cyber policies throughout the enterprise.

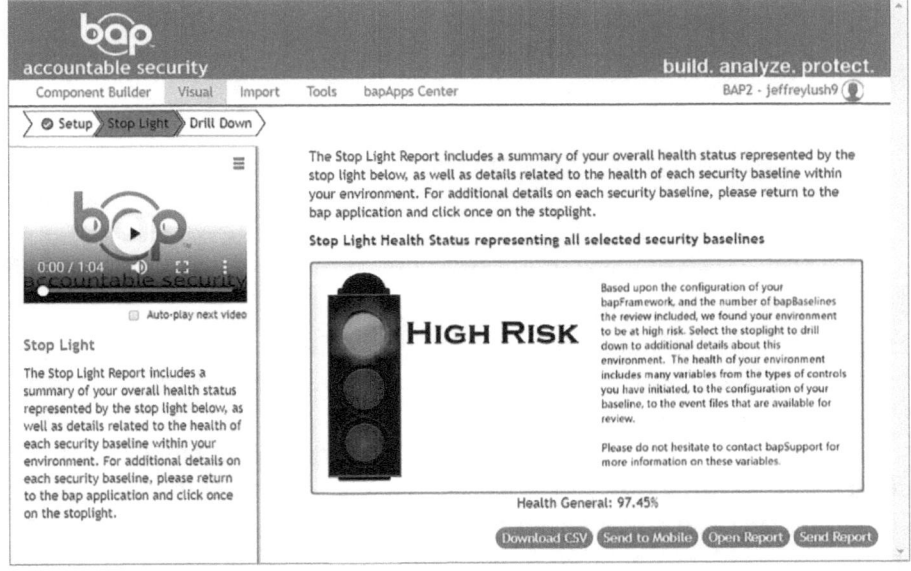

screenshot 3

Based on actual events occurring within the environment, BAP provides "drill-down" functionality to quickly understand the threat.

The stoplight immediately greets you with your level of risk in the environment. Illustrated a screenshot 3, the health of this environment is 97.45% (lower middle of the screen). 100% represents many challenges in the environment. A yellow or green light are always preferred to a red light that indicates high risk.

Included on the screen all of the events and risk can be downloaded into a CSV file, sent to a mobile device or a report is available for viewing and sending to others.

Upon selecting the stoplight, you will be able to inspect the policies that comprise the security rating as seen in screenshot 4 on the next page.

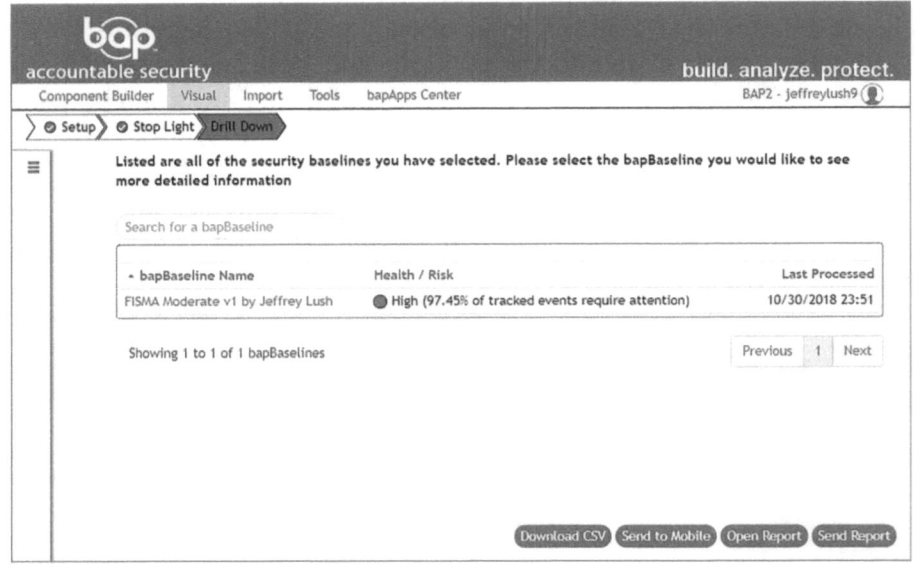

screenshot 4

The drill down screen, as illustrated in screenshot for, displays all baselines that contributed to the report. Found in screenshot 4 is a single baseline "FISMA moderate", although the screen could easily contain hundreds of baselines.

For the Department of Veterans Affairs, you could have a baseline comprised of all VISNS, VAMCs, CBOCs and a centralized report showing the health of the entire Department of Veterans Affairs to include VHA, VBA and NCA and delivered via email daily (example screenshot 5).

Challenge 3 within the VA

- "…security deficiencies were not incorporated into POA&M management and risk management activities in a timely manner."
- "Department had approximately 8,500 open POA&Ms in FY 2017."

BAP can help with Challenge 3

- POA&Ms are automatically create based on actual events.
- Events can be remediated on multiple POA&Ms at one time.

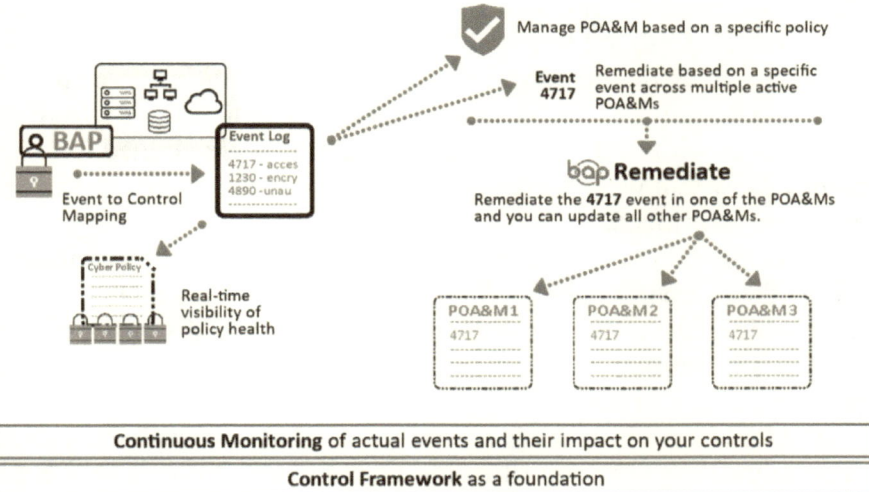

drawing 3

Remediation of events in the environment are not just isolated to the ability to resolve the issue. Documentation of the event is essential to tracking the event to resolution, although with enterprise the size of the Department of Veterans Affairs tracking of events can be a substantial challenge.

There are several interrelated challenges with remediation of events that BAP can assist with.

Identification of the event: Critical to resolving events is the ability to identify the event and its correlated impact or collateral damage. NIST has established the world's largest collection of security controls and policies, and through federal regulation agencies like the Department of Veterans Affairs are held accountable to uphold the policies and controls. Although time is invested in development and implementation of these controls and policies, little comfort is obtained in identifying the event and its impact to services provided by the Department of Veterans Affairs.

In many environments' events are handled like a popularity contest in high school. The popular ones get the attention first, regardless of their value or better put, threat to the environment. This behavior is propagated by our inability to identify events and their relationship to services, agency responsibilities or organizations business deliverables.

BAP starts with the identification of the event and its correlation to the controls that have been implemented within the environment. BAP considers this ground 0 of the attack. BAP provides real-time visualization of ground 0 and all associated damage. Identification of the event comes directly from the event log, not in interpretation of event, or a selection of the popular events, the events, directly from the event logs as with in BAP the events and controls are aligned with one another. Now that we have adequately identified the events, the events need to be prioritized.

Prioritization of the event can be based on multiple variables within the Department of Veterans Affairs. Understanding the relationship of the event to specific ATO's within the VA, broken down by specific controls can provide great value to addressing the most important events first.

POA&M and Remediation: now that we have identified the event which allowed for the prioritization of the event, we can now begin remediation of the event. In most environments, hardware and software is shared in support of the ATO's. As events come into the environment, their impact can affect multiple ATO's. The POA&M is the "paperwork" to managing events to resolution. The POA&Ms for the Department of Veterans Affairs is approximately 8,500 open in 2017. Of those 8,500, it is assumed that many of them share similar events and remediation tasks. This is common practice for federal agencies, as the events are logged based upon the ATO, and since over 50% of the controls supporting the ATO are shared among all ATO's, an event could get logged thousands of times in individual POA&Ms.

this reality creates an enormous workload for the US Department of Veterans Affairs, as well as any other agency.

BAP provides a solution called bapRemediate, which can be displayed and results exported in the POA&M format and spreadsheet as needed. There are several advantages to using bapRemediate for POA&M management.

- As illustrated in drawing 3, event 4717 can be found in many of the POA&Ms in the environment. Built upon the control foundation and continuous monitoring that BAP provides, once event 4717 is remediated, BAP will prompt to propagate the resolution to all POA&Ms with the 4717 event. This technology in and of itself will close thousands of POA&Ms within the Department of Veterans Affairs.

- The POA&M is generated based upon actual events occurring within the environment, not a summary or "spot checking" of the environment. The result is a robust security posture for the entire US Department of Veterans Affairs.

Additional Challenges within the US Department of Veterans Affairs as summary statements.

VA Challenge A

"2. DHS uses data to assist in its oversight responsibilities and to prepare an annual report to Congress on agency compliance with FISMA."

"4. VA continues to face significant challenges in complying with the requirements of FISMA due to the nature and maturity of its information security program. Bullet 1: address security related issues that contributed to the information technology material weakness report in the FY 2017 audit of VA's consolidated financial statements; bullet 2: improve deployment of security patches, system upgrades, and system configurations…; Bullet 3: improve performance monitoring to ensure controls are operating as intended at all facilities and communicate identified security deficiencies to the appropriate personnel so they can take corrective actions to mitigate significant security risks"

BAP Solution A:

BAP provides both proactive and reactive visibility to meet all of the high-level issues outlined leveraging automation and artificial intelligence.

Compliance with FISMA standards is a core strength found within BAP. Extending the core strength to understand the deployment of security patches, upgrades, and configurations allow an organization to identify risk deficiencies and take corrective actions quickly.

Additional details follow as the OIG report goes into material weaknesses and opportunities for improvement.

VA Challenge B:

"We assessed VA's information security program through inquiries, observations, and tests of selected control supporting 44 major applications and general support systems at 24 VA facilities"

BAP Solution B:

Standard in the industry is to perform "spot/selected" tests, analysis for all controls implemented can be a daunting task. With BAP though, review of all controls, policies, and applications is included by default, as artificial intelligence is used to process and provide information.

VA Challenge C:
"1. Agency-wide security management program,
2. Identity management and access controls,
3. Configuration management controls,
4. System development/change management controls,
5. Contingency planning,
6. Incident response and monitoring,
7. Continuous monitoring,
8. Contractor system oversight."
VA Solution C:
BAP helps with the following:
1. Agency wide security management program: BAP is an agency-wide security management program that allows an agency to develop, manage and continually monitor the health and viability of all controls, baselines, and policies deployed within an agency. BAP works as an enterprise application providing local virtual appliances to a centralized distribution model.
2. Identity management and access controls,
3. Configuration management controls,
4. System development/change management controls. The BAP framework allows an agency to manage all levels of controls, their implementation and continually monitor the viability of their application. Additionally, BAP provides validation during the implementation process, providing a highly distributed organization to standardize control distribution in a repeatable and sustainable model quickly.
6. Incident response and monitoring,
7. Continuous monitoring. By default, BAP provides continuous monitoring of all security controls, ATO's, baselines and policies. BAP uniquely leverages existing event logs and analyzes their impact on established controls.
8. Contractor systems oversight. BAP is not restricted to traditional event logs and provides technical and non-technical accountability and validation.

VA Challenge D:

"In agency-wide information security risk management program. VA still faces challenges implementing components of its agency-wide information security risk management program to meet FISMA requirements. Consequently, this audit identified continuing significant deficiencies related to access controls, configuration and management controls, change management controls, and service continuity practices designed to protect mission-critical systems from unauthorized access, alteration, or destruction."

BAP Solution D:

BAP provides a consistent control management infrastructure with NIST 800-53 at its core.

VA Challenge E:

"The ECST has launched 31 plans of action to address previously identified security weakness and the IT material weakness. The ECST has also reported progress to the chief information officer on a weekly basis to ensure corrective actions are tracked and monitored."

BAP Solution E:

BAP provides continuous monitoring of all controls and policies, as well as an automated POA&M output for simplified visibility.

BAP delivers specific control reporting which significantly enhances an organization's ability to drive action and accountability.

VA Challenge F:

"Continued maturation of an IT governance, risk, and compliance tool to improve processes for assessing, authorizing, and monitoring the security posture of VA systems."

BAP Solution F:

BAP provides the only software application that will monitor and assess control and compliance health with real-time events occurring within the environment. BAP can be deployed as a virtual appliance requiring minimal virtual resources (16 GB of RAM and 4 cores of processing) and integrate with existing log aggregation or collect log information natively. BAP provides a central enterprise model distributed to local facilities natively within the BAP framework.

VA Challenge G:
"We continue to see information system security deficiencies similar in type and risk level to our findings in prior years and an overall inconsistent implementation of the security program... VA needs to ensure a proven process is in place across the agency... Continue to address deficiencies it exists within access and configuration management control across all facilities"

BAP Solution G:
The core of BAP allows an enterprise to manage security deficiencies and deploy, manage security controls throughout the organization. BAP provides accountability for both technical and non-technical controls to create consistency across the entire agency.

VA Challenge H:
"... Risk assessments it did not address potential external attacks, human error, previously identified security weaknesses, or significant threat sources such as risks associated with systems not managed by the office of information and technology (OI&T)."

BAP Solution H:
BAP provides validation for both technical and non-technical controls. The unique attribute of BAP software is the ability to align ongoing real-time threat through the analysis of event logs to established controls and policies. Integration with log aggregation products, for example, Splunk are included as well.

VA Challenge I:
"We also identified issues related to the inaccurate reporting of the status for certain system security controls, and noted that two systems were granted authority to operate without undergoing an assessment of security controls"

BAP Solution I:
BAP provides continuous monitoring of all controls and policies. ATO health would have been immediately identified with BAP.

VA Challenge J:

"8500 open POA&Ms that lacks sufficient documentation to justify closure and action items that missed major milestone date...POA&M items that were not updated within the GRC tool to accurately reflect their current status... Not consistently updated to consider all known security weaknesses."

BAP Solution J:

BAP continually evaluates real-time events to all of the controls deployed within policies throughout the organization. As events occur, BAP users can create, manage and complete POA&M activities. Forensic/date range-based reporting is available to evaluate the health of the cyber strategy at any point in time.

VA Challenge K:

"... System security plans with inaccurate information... Inaccurately reported the status of certain security controls..."

BAP Solution K:

BAP allows the organization to manage the implementation of all controls related to policies. bapValidate provides organizations with the ability to validate the information collected within the system security plan meets the centralized organization's objectives.

VA Challenge L:

"We also identified inconsistent monitoring of access and production environments for individuals with excessive privileges within certain major applications... Monitor for instances of unauthorized system access or excessive permissions."

BAP Solution L:

BAP can capture events related to unauthorized access and align them to security controls throughout the environment in real-time.

VA Challenge M:

"VA did not consistently review security violations and audit logs supporting mission-critical systems. Audit log collections and reviews are critical for evaluating security-related activities, such as determining individual accountability, reconstructing security events, detecting intruders, and identifying system performance issues.

Moreover, we have identified and reported deficiencies with audit logging for more than 10 years in our annual FISMA reports."

BAP Solution M:

A key attribute of BAP is the alignment of audit logs, whether the audit log comes from the native source or from a log aggregator or SIEM, BAP uniquely provides visibility in a continuous monitoring model.

VA Challenge N:

"… Could allow any database user to gain excessive unauthorized access permissions to critical system information… Unsecured database configuration settings can allow any database user to gain unauthorized access to critical system information."

BAP Solution N:

All database environments produce access events. Leveraging this event log, BAP can provide visibility as to when access to data structures occurs, and the frequency of that occurrence.

VA Challenge O:

"VA has not implemented effective controls to identify and remediate security weaknesses associated with outdated third-party applications or operating system software."

BAP Solution O:

BAP provides the ability to align audit logs to controls to discover security weaknesses and outdated third-party applications or operating systems.

VA Challenge P:

"… Deficiencies in VA's patch and vulnerability management program could allow malicious users to gain unauthorized access… VA could more effectively remediate vulnerabilities identified and operating systems, databases, applications, and other network devices."

BAP Solution P:

BAP provides multiple alternatives for managing vulnerabilities from patch management reporting and health status to customized data calls and compliance validation methodologies.

VA Challenge Q:
"... VA needs to strengthen its methodologies for monitoring medical devices and ensuring they are properly segregated from other networks."
BAP Solution Q:
BAP provides medical device/IoT controls and management of events.

VA Challenge R:
"VA developed guidelines to define agency-wide security configuration baselines for major information system components. FISMA section 3544 requires each agency to establish minimally acceptable system configuration requirements and ensure compliance. VA has not fully documented or approved security baseline standards for all of its systems. By not implementing consistent agency-wide configuration management standards for major applications and general support systems, VA is placing critical systems at unnecessary risk or unauthorized access, alteration, or destruction."
BAP Solution R:
BAP provides a flexible enterprise-level management tool that enables organizations to quickly inherit controls and policies. BAP enables the creation, management, and inheritance of controls to multiple policies while providing a jumpstart methodology that has most agencies functional in less than 60 minutes.

VA Challenge S:
"However, deficiencies were noted in several areas including to security event monitoring, security event correlation... vulnerability scan monitoring and data exfiltration safeguards."
BAP Solution S:
BAP provides alignment of events to implemented security controls. BAP can aggregate log files natively or receive output from common industry log aggregation tools, like Splunk.

VA Challenge T:

"Specifically, we noted that VA has 12 business partner external conditions that are not currently monitored by one of its trusted Internet connection gateways. We noted that the VA's network and security operations Center was unable to perform adequate security testing of all systems across the enterprise. Ineffective monitoring of internal network segments could prevent VA from detecting and responding to intrusion attempts in a timely manner. As a result, our audit continues to identify numerous high-risk security incidents, including malware infections that were not responded to in a timely manner. Specifically, we noted these issues at for major data centers, 11 VA medical centers, 3 regional offices, and the insurance center. While VA's performance has improved from the prior year the process for tracking, updating, and closing security-related incidents was not performed consistently throughout the year."

BAP Solution T:

BAP provides accountability for all implemented security policies, baselines and ATO's. BAP uniquely provides this visibility based upon the health of the implemented security control and can extend to non-technical controls as well. System testing is continuous within BAP. The continuous monitoring capability within BAP balances cyber requirements with large organizations that require agility, like the VA.

VA Challenge U:

"VA has implemented several tools including "Splunk" and "qRadar" to facilitate enhanced audit log collection and analysis... The tools did not collect data from all critical systems and major applications. Network security and operation center did not have full visibility to evaluate all security-related audit data throughout the enterprise for the entire year. Management plans to fully implement the "Splunk" tool across all platforms in support of an agency-wide security incident and event management solution."

BAP Solution U:

For an enterprise the size of the Department of Veterans Affairs, an agency-wide log aggregation tool is an absolute step in the right direction. Although the collection of log information is valuable, if the VA would like to understand the security posture of the agency, the VA will need to align actual events occurring in the environment with the establish security controls and policies. BAP helps log aggregators understand specific events to monitor during the initial set up and maintenance of log aggregator while aligning the actual events occurring in the environment to establish the health of the controls implemented.

VA Challenge V:
"FISMA section 3544 requires each agency to develop and implement an agency-wide information security program containing specific procedures for detecting, reporting, and responding to computer security incidents. We performed for unannounced scans of internal networks, and despite federal regulations for detecting this type of activity, none of the scans were blocked by the network security and operation center."

BAP Solution V:
BAP provides visibility as to events occurring within the environment. BAP will provide visibility that the scans were occurring allowing the network security and operation center to take immediate action.

VA Challenge W:
"VA lacks a comprehensive continuous monitoring program to manage information security risks and operations across the enterprise."

BAP Solution W:
BAP is built on the concept of continuous monitoring. The alignment of actual events occurring in the environment to the controls implemented within the environment, provide consumers with immediate feedback as to the viability or health of the controls implemented, providing continuous monitoring of security risk based upon an agencies policy.

Appendix C: BAP Functionality

Appendix C is a collection of BAP functionality illustrated with actual screen shots of the application.

Baseline Summary Report

The Summary Report provides a view of the customers control health for a specific or collection of policies.

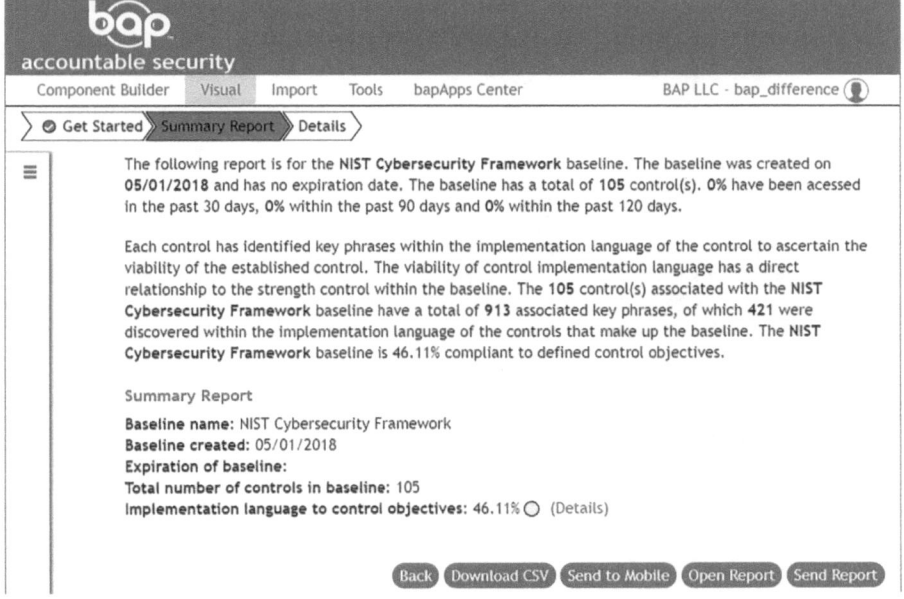

screenshot 5

The summary report can be very helpful for environments that are distributed yet have a centralized responsibility for compliance. Distribution of controls and policies to a large organization can be very challenging to drive accountability.

With BAP, frameworks are distributed throughout the enterprise, where centralized controls and policies can be easily distributed, while providing maximum flexibility for individual site implementation if desired. The summary report illustrated in screenshot 5 allows an organization to monitor the progress of a site and their compliance to a specific policy, control, or group of policies. For example, central office wanted to check on the progress of the Tucson Medical Center. Central office could go in and look at Tucson's progress on their framework. Note some of the details found in screenshot 5 and screenshot 6.

"The baseline has a total of 105 controls. 0% have been accessed in the past 30 days, 0% within the past 90 days, and 0% within the past 120 days": central office distributed the controls and policies to the Tucson office on January 1, over the course of the past 3 months Tucson has not implemented any of the controls distributed to them.

The NIST cyber security framework baseline is 46.11% compliant to defined control objectives: based on actual events occurring with in their environment that was established during the installation, there cyber security health is just over 46%, or moderate.

The following report is for the **NIST Cybersecurity Framework** baseline. The baseline was created on **05/01/2018** and has no expiration date. The baseline has a total of **105** control(s). **0%** have been acessed in the past **30** days, **0%** within the past **90** days and **0%** within the past **120** days.

Each control has identified key phrases within the implementation language of the control to ascertain the viability of the established control. The viability of control implementation language has a direct relationship to the strength control within the baseline. The **105** control(s) associated with the **NIST Cybersecurity Framework** baseline have a total of **913** associated key phrases, of which **421** were discovered within the implementation language of the controls that make up the baseline. The NIST **Cybersecurity Framework** baseline is 46.11% compliant to defined control objectives.

Summary Report

Baseline name: NIST Cybersecurity Framework
Baseline created: 05/01/2018
Expiration of baseline:
Total number of controls in baseline: 105
Implementation language to control objectives: 46.11% ◯ (Details)

screenshot 6

Data Collection

If the data collection has not been validated for accuracy, the data may create an increased workload that may cause the data never to be fully utilized. BAP provides automated data collection and validation:

As a recipient of a data collection request (data call)
As the recipient of the data collection request, they complete their input and are equipped with an instant scoring of their content. The BAP Artificial Intelligence uses a series of key phrases (customizable

by the originator of the data collection request) and searches the provided content. If the key phrase is not found, the recipient is given hints and allowed to modify their submission. The result: The originator receives accurate input, and the recipient gets training on expectations related to the data collection, a real win-win.

Validation of data received for the enterprise
Validation scores are collected by all the data collection requests and forwarded to the enterprise for an enterprise view of the data collection.

Accountability.
Beyond validation of the data collection, BAP enables continuous monitoring of the questions within the collected data that have associated electronic events. BAP provides customers with the following for accountability:

- Use BAP to create a custom control and correlate events within the environment to provide continuous monitoring of the control health.
- Often data collection and certification is a hybrid effort between technical and non-technical data. The BAP framework provides the ability to link all data together for enterprise health.
- The line between data collection and certification and cyber accountability continues to blur. BAP integrates cyber with your data collection and certification efforts, providing a library of over 4,000 controls and several tools.

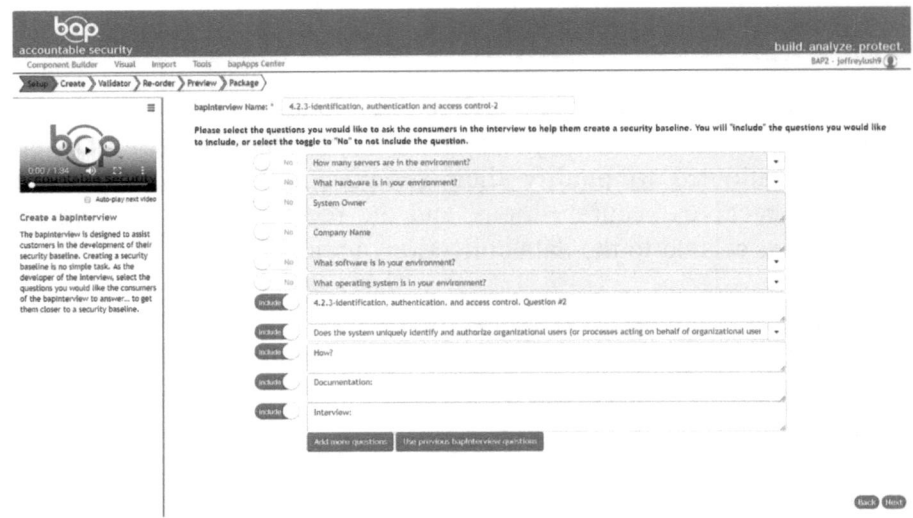

screenshot 7 - customized data collection creation

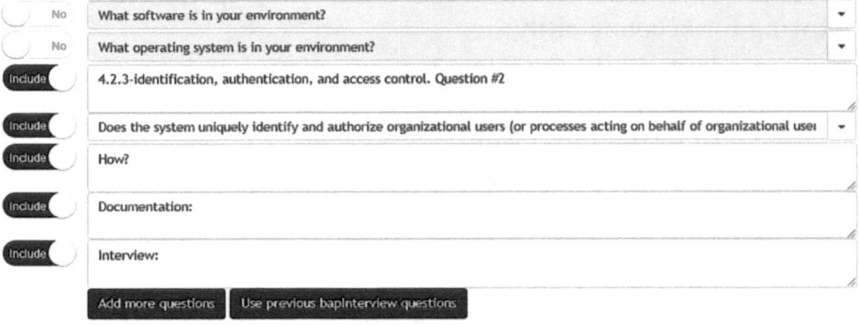

screenshot 8 - (detailed view of screenshot 7)

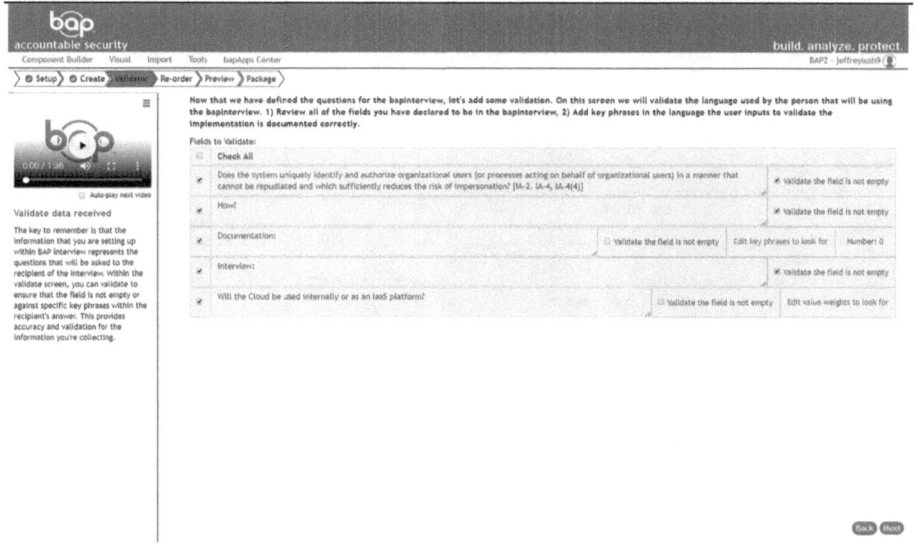

screenshot 9 - validation of interview questions

Fields to Validate:				
☐ Check All				
Does the system uniquely identify and authorize organizational users (or processes acting on behalf of organizational users) in a manner that cannot be repudiated and which sufficiently reduces the risk of impersonation? [IA-2, IA-4, IA-4(4)]	☑ Validate the field is not empty			
How?	☑ Validate the field is not empty			
Documentation:	☐ Validate the field is not empty	Edit key phrases to look for	Number: 0	
Interview:	☑ Validate the field is not empty			
Will the Cloud be used internally or as an IaaS platform?	☐ Validate the field is not empty	Edit value weights to look for		

screenshot 10 - (detailed view of screenshot 9)

BAP Virtual Appliance

The BAP framework installs as a virtual appliance. It can be installed on VMWare or Microsoft hypervisors ranging from the free to cloud versions of the hypervisors.

The configuration of the virtual machine at a minimum 16 GB of RAM, four processor cores. Optimal performance is achieved at 32 GB of RAM, 8 processor cores. Screenshot 11 shows an example of other configuration items as they appear in a VMware workstation configuration.

bapEnterprise is 100% self-contained and will run on any system that meets the minimum specifications. No additional software, no special operating systems or databases, the BAP virtual appliance is exactly what it says-a virtual appliance with no dependencies.

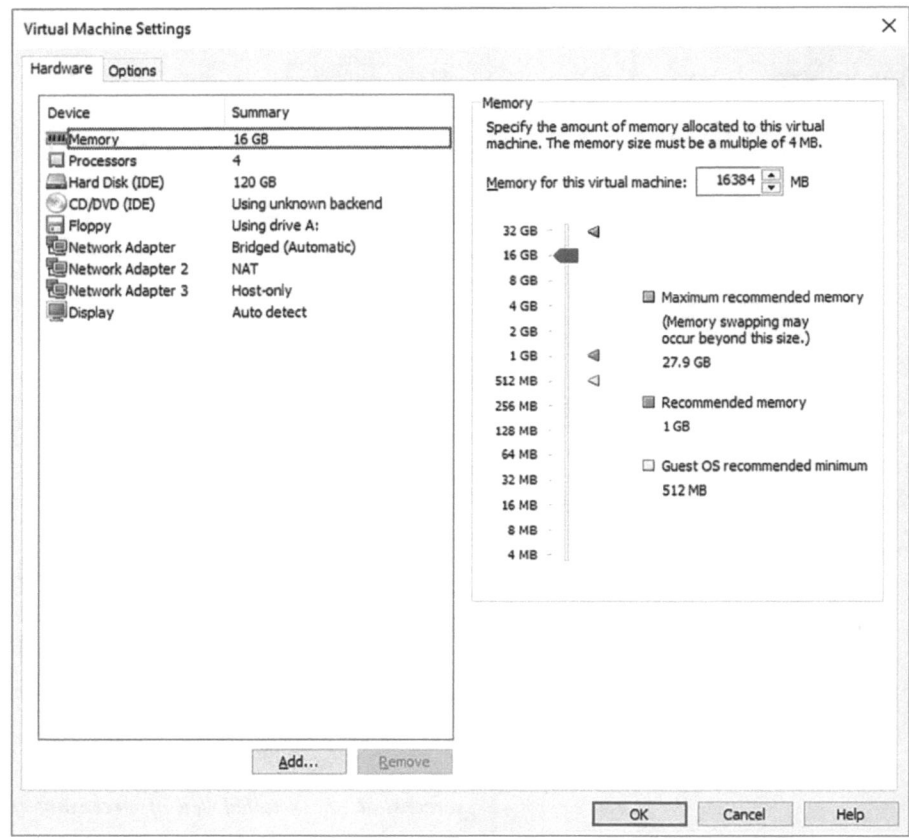

screenshot 11 - BAP virtual appliance configuration

Device	Summary
Memory	16 GB
Processors	4
Hard Disk (IDE)	120 GB
CD/DVD (IDE)	Using unknown backend
Floppy	Using drive A:
Network Adapter	Bridged (Automatic)
Network Adapter 2	NAT
Network Adapter 3	Host-only
Display	Auto detect

screenshot 12 – (detailed view of screenshot 11)

bapCloud OCS

You will start with using bapOCS to build your policies or custom-built them. bapOCS provides you with the opportunity to select from a group of cyber objectives to create the controls and policies needed for your environment. In addition to cyber objectives, you can create controls and policies based on regulatory requirements. Once you have carefully selected the controls you would like to use, pulling from multiple security bodies throughout the industry, you will be presented with the comparison of all policies within bapOCS. For example, you may be looking to enhance your protection of personally identifiable information (PII) and collect 50 controls to satisfy that need. Of those 50 controls, bapOCS will illustrate that 42 of the PII controls also apply to PCI. This allows you to increase your controls by 8, and now have compliance for both PII and PCI.

bapOCS allows you to select from multiple cyber objectives. (see screenshot 13 and 14), the user has selected incident management, the NIST critical infrastructure cybersecurity framework 1.1, and PII. Note the checkmarks are filled in indicating the item has been selected. Also, note underneath the topic objective, the subtext explains the number of sub objectives, which we will see more of on the next screen. Is not uncommon to have subcategories related to control bodies.

The primary objective of the review screen (screenshot 14 and 15) is for you to fine-tune the controls that you will use within your environment. Expect to spend a few minutes on the screen if you are choosing cybersecurity objectives that are not associated with a regulatory requirement. Your fine tuning does not have to be perfect, once the controls of been imported into your framework, you can de-allocate them or delete them if you no longer need them.

bapOCS is a powerful tool for any organization looking to define their cyber needs, all built upon industry standard control bodies.

bap
accountable security

build. analyze. protect.

Objectives Sub-objectives Review Preview Package Delivery

Objective name	Sub-objective name	Control name	Control description	Preview
NIST Critical Infrastructure Cyber Security 1.1	RS.CO	RS.CO-4 (CSF)	Coordination with stakeholders occurs consistent with response plans	
NIST Critical Infrastructure Cyber Security 1.1	RS.CO	RS.CO-5 (CSF)	Voluntary information sharing occurs with external stakeholders to achieve broader cybersecurity sit	
NIST Critical Infrastructure Cyber Security 1.1	RS.IM	RS.IM-1 (CSF)	Response plans incorporate lessons learned	
NIST Critical Infrastructure Cyber Security 1.1	RS.IM	RS.IM-2 (CSF)	Response strategies are updated	
NIST Critical Infrastructure Cyber Security 1.1	RS.MI	RS.MI-1 (CSF)	Incidents are contained	
NIST Critical Infrastructure Cyber Security 1.1	RS.MI	RS.MI-2 (CSF)	Incidents are mitigated	
NIST Critical Infrastructure Cyber Security 1.1	RS.MI	RS.MI-3 (CSF)	Newly identified vulnerabilities are mitigated or documented as accepted risks	
PII (800-53-J)*	access control	AR-7	Least access privilege for individuals through the development of privacy controls. (NIST 800-53: A	
PII (800-53-J)*	access control	DI-2	Establishes process and accountability for the integrity of PII data through the use of security con	
PII (800-53-J)*	access control	DI-2(1)	Publish of computer matching agreements on the organization's public website. (NIST 800-53: SC-8, SC	

screenshot 14 - review the controls selected by OCS

ives Sub-objectives Review Preview Package Delivery

Objective name	Sub-objective name	Control name	Control description
NIST Critical Infrastructure Cyber Security 1.1	RS.CO	RS.CO-4 (CSF)	Coordination with stakeh with response plans
NIST Critical Infrastructure Cyber Security 1.1	RS.CO	RS.CO-5 (CSF)	Voluntary information sh stakeholders to achieve l
NIST Critical Infrastructure Cyber Security 1.1	RS.IM	RS.IM-1 (CSF)	Response plans incorpora
NIST Critical Infrastructure Cyber Security 1.1	RS.IM	RS.IM-2 (CSF)	Response strategies are u
NIST Critical Infrastructure Cyber Security 1.1	RS.MI	RS.MI-1 (CSF)	Incidents are contained

screenshot 15 - detailed view of screenshot 14

Importing BAP Components

BAP is designed so that users can easily import information from other BAP users. Imagine Central office creating all the controls and policies and you simply import and began monitoring.

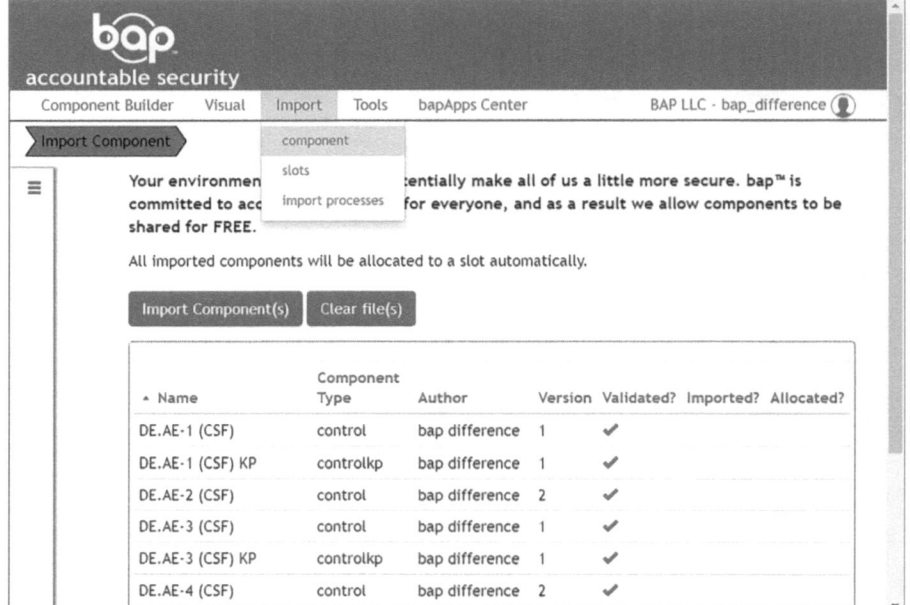

Create customized controls

Instead of using bapOCS, you may want to create your controls from scratch or modify pre-existing controls (over 4,000) that come by default with BAP. Building a control allows you to define "what right looks like". A control provides an objective that can be monitored and consistent throughout the organization. There are multiple attributes when authoring a control:

- The weight of the control allows us to be very specific as to the impact of variables that might threaten the effectiveness of the control. A common weight is 10.
- The control body allows you to organize your controls in bodies. Like NIST or ISO.

- The control description is a brief description of the control objective whereas the control language is the detailed description.
- You can choose to import controls from other controls, and should take the time to associate control key phrases with the controls.
- The implementation language is the expectation of how the control will be implemented and is typically provided as a generic set of guidance to be modified during the implementation of the control as it relates to the policy objective.

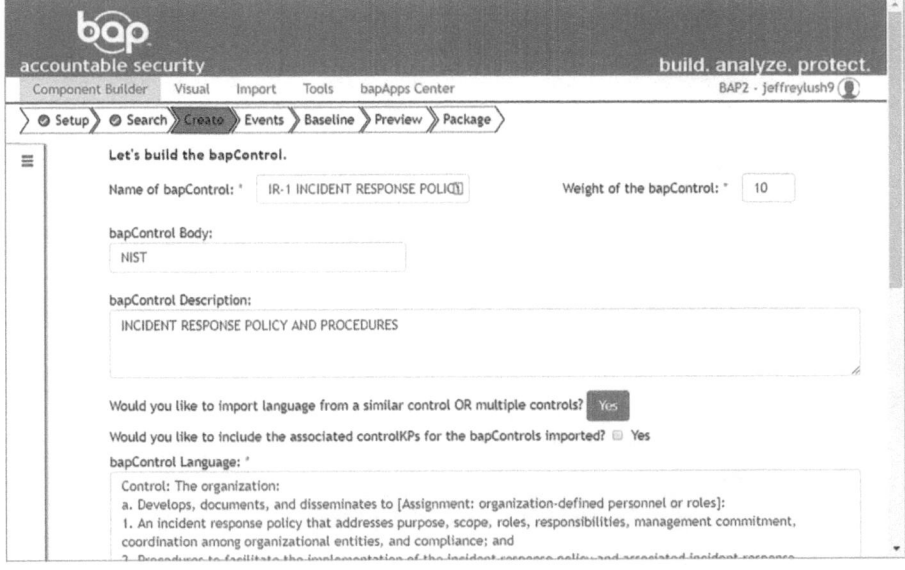

screenshot 17 - create controls

Every control has an associated set of key phrases. The concept of a key phrase is not foreign in the industry. In the 1950s speed-reading was introduced to the world which uses the idea of "skimming and scanning" to ascertain the content being read. The concept of speed-reading is used as a core component of most artificial intelligence leveraging algorithms and a complex set of meta tags. BAP implemented key phrases several years before the cyber industry recognized the strength of key phrases, illustrated in the soon to be released NIST 800-53, rev 5.

Within BAP, key phrases are associated with both the controls and the events, which assist in BAP's unique ability to ascertain the health of the control and ultimately policy. We will discuss within the controlKP chapter how you can modify, create and add weighted values to key phrases within your environment. BAP has preconfigured thousands of controls with key phrases so that you can get started immediately, fine-tuning over the course of time.

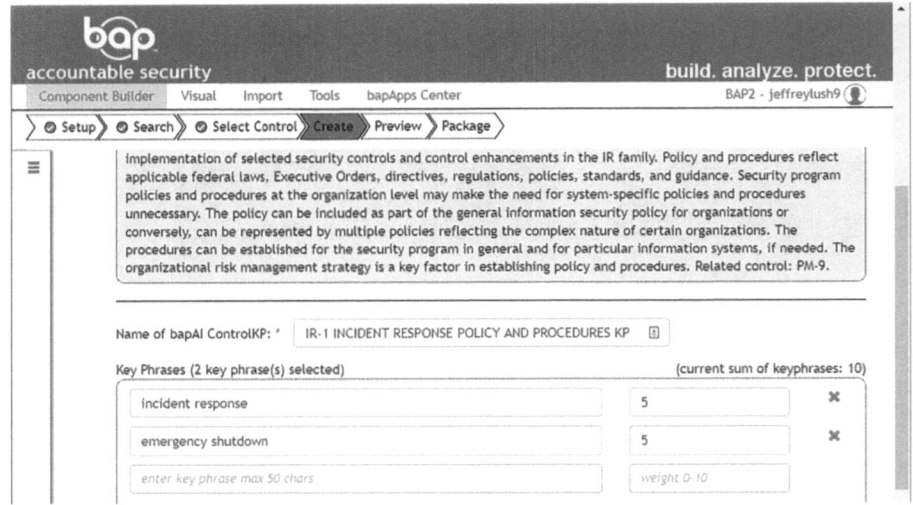

screenshot 18 - create control key phrases

screenshot 19 - (detailed view of screenshot 18)

Align controls with event logs

The event logs produced by hardware and software within our environment provide a wealth of information regarding the actual health of our environment. The industry has invested billions of dollars developing software on analyzing the information from multiple event logs within the infrastructure to ultimately find that needle in a haystack.

The use of log aggregators and SIEM products have greatly enhanced our ability to find that needle in the haystack, allowing us to author scripts and algorithms to discover the threat to our environment. Over the course of time industries recognized great value in these products, although the effort required often exceeds that of the conventional IT administrator.

Let's assume that we have 20 different components within our environment, remember a component defined hardware or software like network firewalls, operating systems, applications, and databases. Establishing a cyber strategy requires the implementation of cyber standards, often referred to as controls. The cyber standards include access to your system, encryption, insider threat, and a myriad of other cyber standards. For this example, let's assume there are 100 cyber standards.

With 20 different components and 100 standards, what is the probable impact of an event to those controls? The firewall is breached which had a direct effect on the access control standard, using 10 as high risk, let's assign a 9 to this breach. Because of the breached firewall, my LDAP server which typically a risk of 1, now has an elevated risk of 4, due to the breach in the firewall. We understand there are 20 different components, although what are the total potential events per component? Your router may have 5,000 possible events. We have only discussed the impact of a single event code and the relationship of that single event to components within our environment.

The use of SIEM or log aggregators can undoubtedly reduce the number of events to be processed, although the mathematical algorithms needed to understand the risk level impact is very complicated, based on the staggering potential implications and varying levels of impact.

The BAP framework is a simple to use artificial general intelligence that enables the mapping of the real-time threat to natural language. When an event occurs, the bapAI searches for impact and within minutes delivers results of how that cyber breach impacted all the components and standards within your environment.

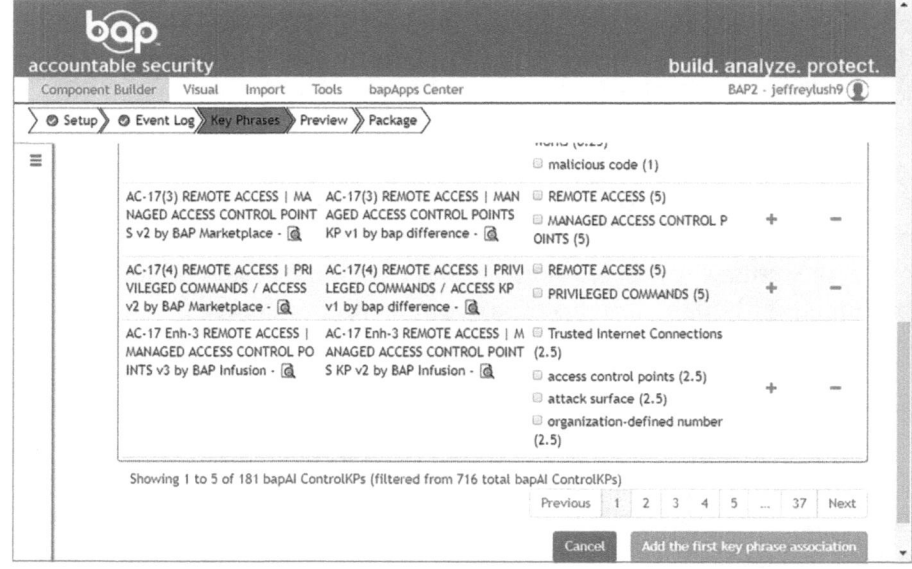

screenshot 20 - aligning controls and events

AC-17(3) REMOTE ACCESS | MA NAGED ACCESS CONTROL POINT S v2 by BAP Marketplace -	AC-17(3) REMOTE ACCESS | MAN AGED ACCESS CONTROL POINTS KP v1 by bap difference -	REMOTE ACCESS (5) MANAGED ACCESS CONTROL P OINTS (5)	**+**	**—**
AC-17(4) REMOTE ACCESS | PRI VILEGED COMMANDS / ACCESS v2 by BAP Marketplace -	AC-17(4) REMOTE ACCESS | PRIVI LEGED COMMANDS / ACCESS KP v1 by bap difference -	REMOTE ACCESS (5) PRIVILEGED COMMANDS (5)	**+**	**—**
AC-17 Enh-3 REMOTE ACCESS | MANAGED ACCESS CONTROL PO INTS v3 by BAP Infusion -	AC-17 Enh-3 REMOTE ACCESS | M ANAGED ACCESS CONTROL POINT S KP v2 by BAP Infusion -	Trusted Internet Connections (2.5) access control points (2.5) attack surface (2.5) organization-defined number (2.5)	**+**	**—**

screenshot 21 - (detailed view of screenshot 20)

Creating policies

The time has come for all organizations to align with a cybersecurity baseline and begin the journey to accountability. I know for some organizations this may seem like an undaunting task, as frequently the requirements are issued by individuals that understand the cyber outcomes they desire, although may struggle to communicate the actionable requirements. If you are reading and think "This has not happened to me yet," I suggest you may want to look at a few of the regulations throughout the globe that may impact your business/organization. A few examples:

- If you are conducting business in the EU (Europe block) you will need to be compliant with GDPR, which is PII on steroids.
- If you plan to perform work for the US DoD, DFARS should be top of mind. And for the Civilian and Intelligence segments in the US Government... I am confident a DFARS like regulation is coming, so do not feel left out.
- If you plan to move money through the State of New York (which includes many organizations), look at 23 NYCRR 500.
- If you are feeling left out and you are required to be compliant with the US Security Exchange Commission (SEC), lots of new requirements.

I have only mentioned a few of the hottest security baselines; the list shares company with FISMA, FedRAMP, HIPAA, NERC, PII, PCI-DSS, GLBA, PHI, RMF, CSF and many others.

It is important to recognize there is a shift in the industry from "compliance" to "accountable security." Compliance does not always mean that you are secure and without risk. When developing your cyber strategy a few suggestions:

1. You are not alone and do not have to start from ground zero. NIST, specifically NIST 800-53 provides the world's most complete set of security controls that will align with the security objectives you are trying to meet. Use the NIST 800-53 controls as a starting point and modify for your environment. I know BAP has developed tools to review requirements like GDPR, SEC and 23 NYCRR 500, etc..

aligning the cyber objectives/requirements to suggested NIST 800-53 controls, making life a lot easier.

2. Establishing security controls that are easily scalable to multiple security policies. Build your new security controls based on existing controls or NIST 800-53 controls... again, let's keep it simple.

3. Many of the new requirements have associated penalties for non-compliance. With established controls grouped into policy, let's go ahead and add accountability. With BAP you can easily measure real-time threat to declare the integrity/effectiveness of the controls you have deployed.

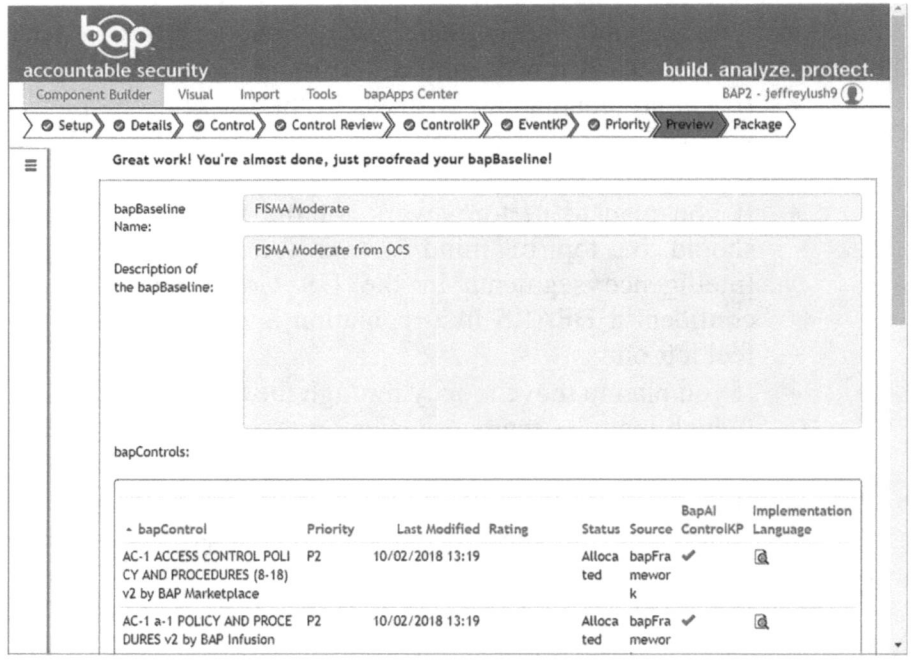

screenshot 22 - developing a policy with controls you have created

Custom Implementation Language

The controls within your framework should stay consistent as they clearly define objectives for your environment, although the implementation of your controls should maintain complete flexibility, as every control will impact policies in unique ways.

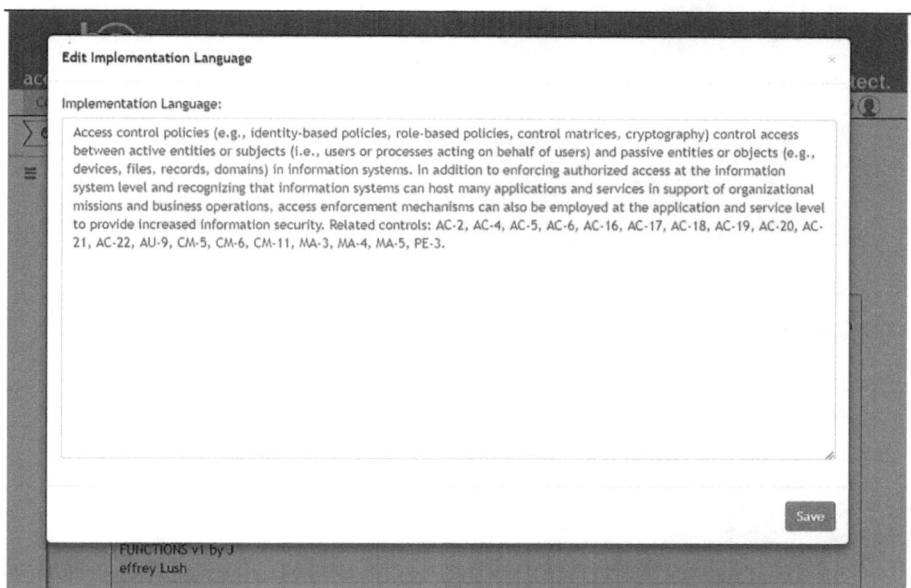

Edit Implementation Language

Implementation Language:

Access control policies (e.g., identity-based policies, role-based policies, control matrices, cryptography) control access between active entities or subjects (i.e., users or processes acting on behalf of users) and passive entities or objects (e.g., devices, files, records, domains) in information systems. In addition to enforcing authorized access at the information system level and recognizing that information systems can host many applications and services in support of organizational missions and business operations, access enforcement mechanisms can also be employed at the application and service level to provide increased information security. Related controls: AC-2, AC-4, AC-5, AC-6, AC-16, AC-17, AC-18, AC-19, AC-20, AC-21, AC-22, AU-9, CM-5, CM-6, CM-11, MA-3, MA-4, MA-5, PE-3.

Save

screenshot 23 - implementation language per policy

Share Components

BAP is designed so that users can easily share information with other BAP users. Imagine designing the perfect set of controls and policies at Central Office and distributing the files to the entire enterprise.

Sharing components allows an organization to truly propagate their cyber strategy quickly, consistently, and in the repeatable manner. Cross agencies can share best practices, and policies and controls can be developed in a much more rapid pace, allowing organizations to apply the controls to become more secure in their environments.

Sharing of components is free. The only requirement is that the recipient of the component is running a bapFramework. When the components are shared they are encrypted, and can only be opened by another bapFramework.

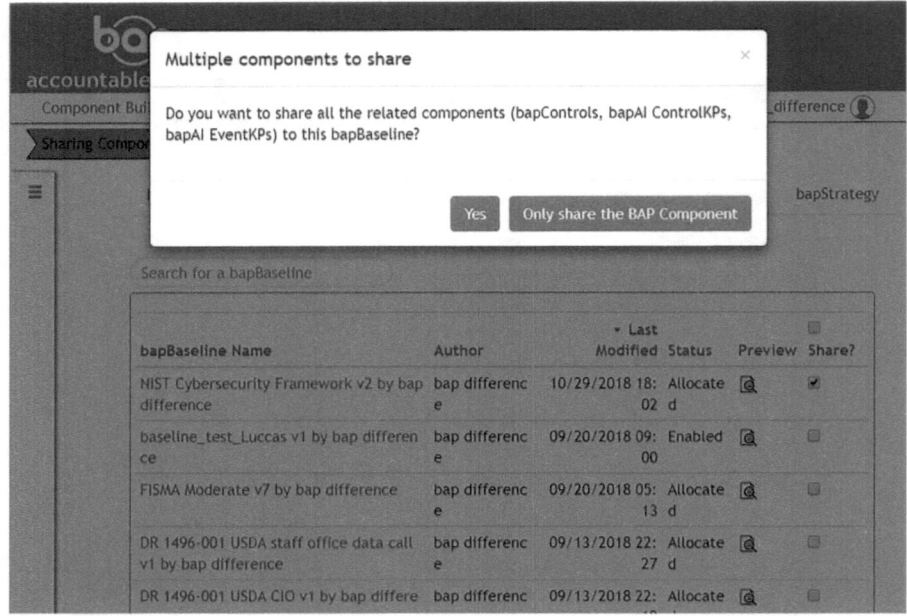

screenshot 24 - sharing a bapBaseline (policy)

Licensing designed to lower cost

BAP licensing is focused on supporting customers to manage unlimited controls and policies, while only charging for controls that are actively part of a policy.

BAP encourages customers to inherit controls among multiple policies to drive down customer cost as the environment becomes more secure. If a control is inherited to multiple policies, the customer only pays for the use of the control one time and can inherit the control to as many policies as needed.

Imagine a software that decreases cost as you become more secure, a real win-win. See screenshot 25 and 26 for illustrations.

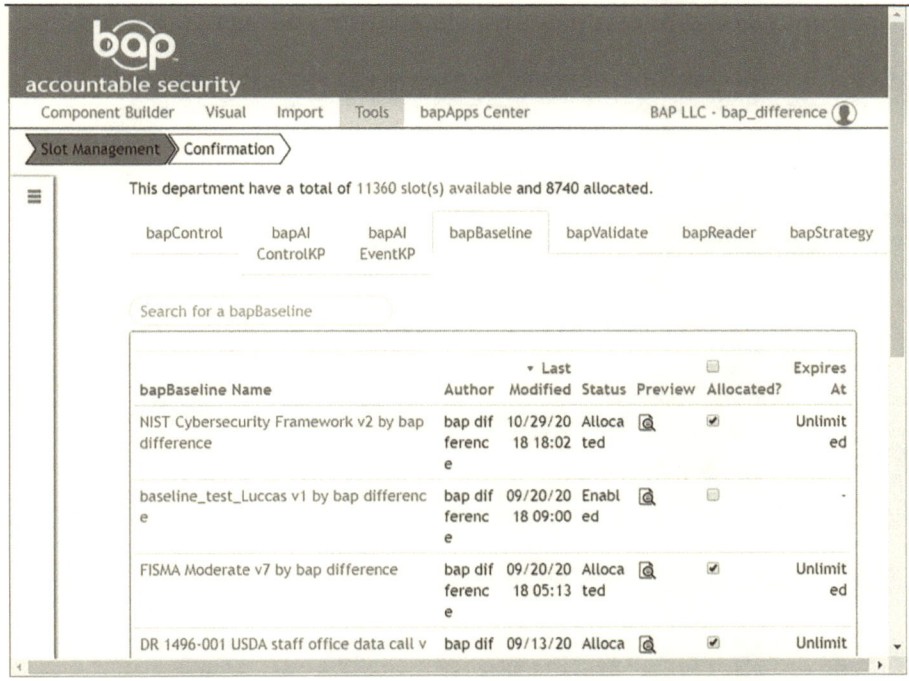

screenshot 25 - allocating slots

| bapControl | bapAI ControlKP | bapAI EventKP | bapBaseline | bapValidate | bapReader | bapStrategy |

Search for a bapBaseline

bapBaseline Name	Author	▾ Last Modified	Status	Preview	☐ Allocated?	Expires At
NIST Cybersecurity Framework v2 by bap difference	bap dif ferenc e	10/29/20 18 18:02	Alloca ted	🔍	☑	Unlimit ed

screenshot 26 - (detailed view of screenshot 25)

BAP VM Management Tool

In the following example, the VM Management tool enables the modification of the IP interface. Additional functionality includes patch updates, rollback, snapshots, backup, recovery and other features designed to keep your bapFramework healthy and current. All imports and patches can be completed with removable media to allow your bapFramework to be completely isolated from your network, if desired.

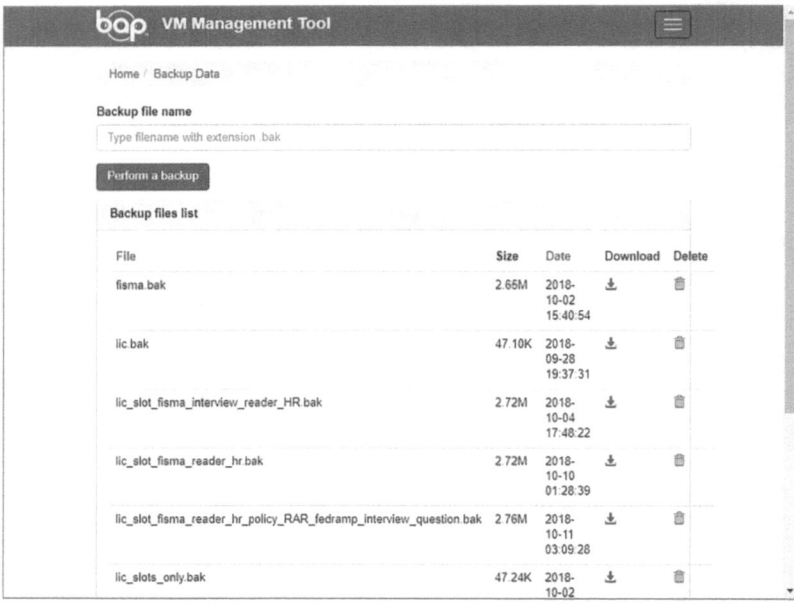

screenshot 27 - vmtools backup and recovery

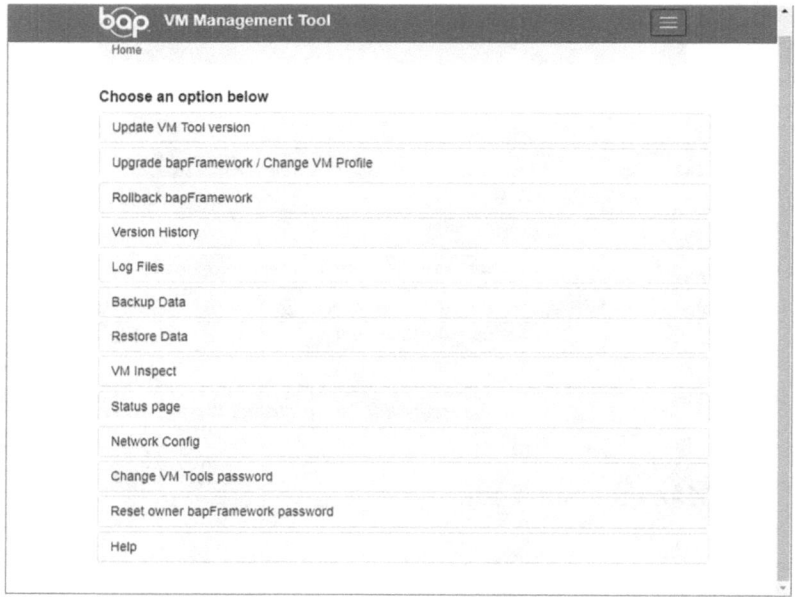

screenshot 28 - vmtools all options

BAP as an Audit Tool

BAP can process baselines and event logs manually (no limit). The process works well for auditors.

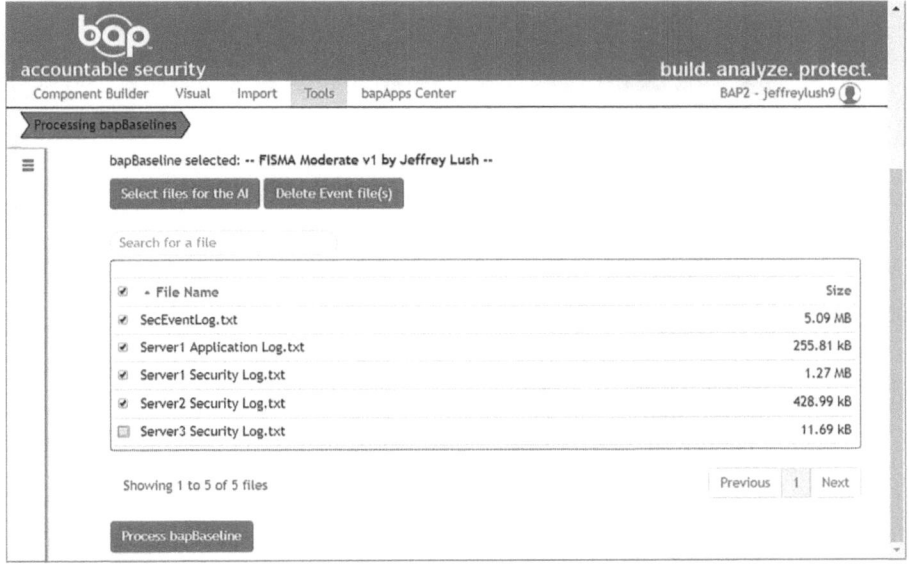

screenshot 29 - select event logs to process against the policy

Remediation

Based on actual events occurring within the environment, users can select to remediate events using bapRemediate.

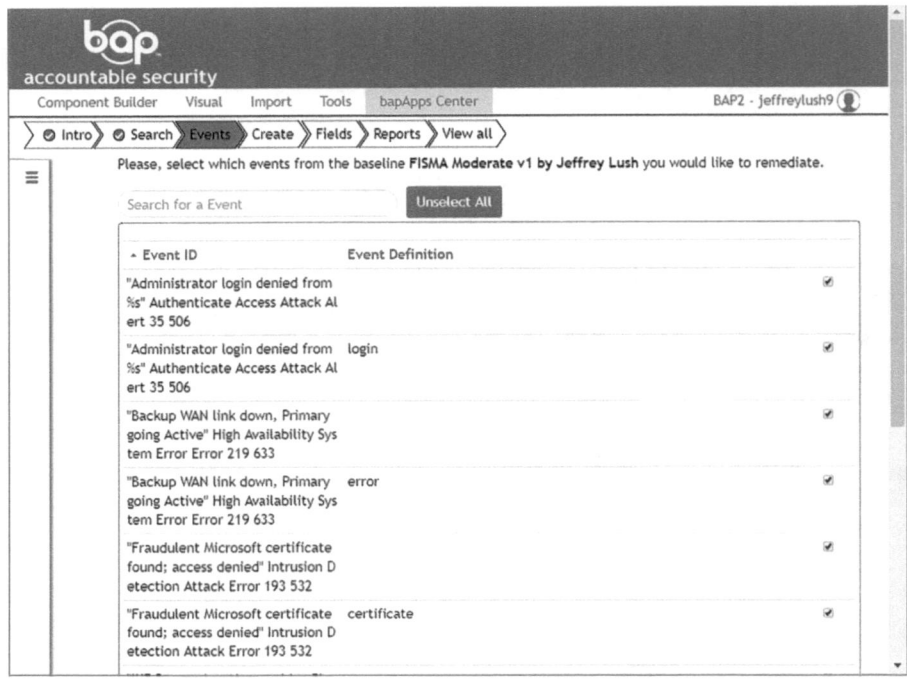

screenshot 30 - select and event to remediate

Glossary

bapValidate, also known as

bapValidate (when consumed)

Establishing standards requires the collection of information, and bapValidate performs that task. bapValidate can be accessed from within the component builder for the team members that are developing the interviews. For the consumption of the bapValidate, is obtained through the BAP apps center as bapValidate, as well as in the BAP QuickStart menu.

bapControl, also known as

cybersecurity control

cybersecurity standard

A standard often referred to as a control which is made up of a stated objective and the implementation of processes and technologies to meet that objective. Within the cybersecurity industry this is referred to as a security control, although can be applied to any number of standards implemented within an organization. bapControl is hosted by the BAP Component Builder and allows organizations to add new, edit, merge, allocate and associate BAP Controls with specific policies.

bapAI ControlKP, also known as

control KP

as discussed, a control includes an objective and the implementation of processes and technology to meet the objective. A unique BAP attribute allows an organization to align real-time threat to established standards. To accomplish this, the bapAI ControlKP is the collection of key phrases (KP) and their associated weights. This information is used as a valuation criterion for the artificial intelligence (AI) running within the bapFramework. The bapAI ControlKP component allows you to create and modify the assigned key phrases to specific standards or bapControls. The bapAI ControlKP is found within the BAP Component Builder.

KP, also known as

Key phrase

A key phrase is in the expression or definition of a standard or event within the organization. Key phrases interpret technical language or industry jargon into natural language. Key phrases are found within any BAP components that leverage the BAP artificial intelligence (bapAI).

Component also known as

slot

A component of the bapFramework is a sub process to achieve a specific task within the bapFramework. Components are created by subject matter experts, general users, and prepackaged components available for download from the bapMarketplace. BAP components fit into a BAP slot.

BAP slot, also known as

a BAP component

The BAP slot enables BAP components to run within the bapFramework. BAP is built upon an open framework, allowing components to be allocated as slots to provide specific services. A bapControl, for example, on encryption is required to meet a business objective. The bapControl that enables encryption is established in a slot. Slot licenses are imported using the bapFramework import menu, whereas the management of the slots is found within the tools menu of the bapFramework. Slots can be purchased through the bapMarketplace.

bapAI EventKP, also known as

event KP

Understanding real-time threat detection requires the use of event logs and traps. The event logs are populated with specific event codes and key phrases. The interpretation of the event codes and their relationship to the multiple standards within the environment is accomplished within the bapAI EventKP. The bapAI EventKP works in conjunction with the bapAI ControlKP to establish near real-time threat. The bapAI EventKP can be managed using the component builder.

bapBaseline
security policy

A bapBaseline is a collection of standards to meet specific organization and business objectives. The BAP standard provides a consistent collection of standards that are often applied to multiple baselines or policies. The objective of this standard stays consistent, although the implementation of the standard may vary depending upon the policy. The BAP Component Builder enables organizations to create, edit and manage their baselines and policies. Each bapBaseline consumes a single slot although the variance of the policy specific implementation of the slot consuming standard does not consume a slot as it is specific to the policy. The impact of a specific standard as it relates to specific policies is adjusted using priorities within the development of the bapBaseline.

BAP QuickCheck

BAP QuickCheck is a simple tool that allows users to enter in three key phrases and search up to three documents at a time. BAP QuickCheck is found within the bapApps Center as well as bapsolution.com. BAP QuickCheck illustrates the strength of the BAP artificial intelligence, without all of the detail associated with bapReader and bapValidate. Following a successful QuickCheck, BAP provides the number of times a specific keyword and key phrase was discovered within the selected documents BAP QuickCheck is a free BAP tool that is part of the bapFramework.

bapVisual
bapVisual hosts the dashboard and reports.

Process baseline

The process baseline function is part of the tools menu within the bapFramework. Process baseline allows organizations to establish policies and test the policies in real time for effectiveness.

Document ideas about your Strategy

www.ingramcontent.com/pod-product-compliance
Lightning Source LLC
Chambersburg PA
CBHW030907180526
45163CB00004B/1737